THE ULTIMATE BOOK OF
PHONICS WORD LISTS
FOR GRADES 1–2

Word, Phrase, and Sentence Lists, Plus Games
for Reading, Writing, and Word Study

LAURIE J. COUSSEAU AND RHONDA GRAFF

DEDICATION

To Joann Crawford, my mentor who taught me everything
I know about linguistic structure and who transformed
the lives of so many children and educators
— L. C.

To my very special friends, Holly and Jackie,
with love and appreciation
— R. G.

Thank you to our editor, Maria Chang,
for her support and guidance.

SVP & Publisher: Tara Welty
Editor: Maria L. Chang
Creative director: Tannaz Fassihi
Cover design: Cynthia Ng
Interior design: Maria Lilja
Images © Shutterstock.com and The Noun Project.

ISBN: 978-1-5461-1268-6

CONTENTS

INTRODUCTION 5

Glossary of Phonetic Terms 9

WORD, PHRASE, AND SENTENCE LISTS

Soft *c* /s/ 11

Soft *g* /j/ 14

/j/ Spelled *-dge* 17

Y as a Vowel

y Pronounced /ī/ 19

    y Pronounced /ĭ/ 20

y Pronounced /ē/ 21

    Suffix *-y* 22

    Suffix *-ly* 24

Vowel Teams

Long *a* /ā/ Spelled *ai, ay* 26

Long *a* /ā/ Spelled *eigh, ei, ey, ea* 30

Long *e* /ē/ Spelled *ee, ea* 32

    Short *e* /ĕ/ Spelled *ea* 37

Long *e* /ē/ Spelled *ey, ie, ei* 39

Long *i* /ī/ Spelled *igh* 41

Long *i* /ī/ Spelled *ie, y_e* 43

Long *o* /ō/ Spelled *oa, ow* 45

Long *o* /ō/ Spelled *oe, ou* 49

Long *u* /ū/ and Long *oo* /o͞o/ Spelled *ew, ue* ... 50

Long *oo* /o͞o/ Spelled *ou, ui* 52

Long-Vowel Spelling Patterns: *-ild, -ind, -old, -olt, -ost* ... 53

r-Controlled Vowels

r-Controlled Vowel *ar* /är/ 55

r-Controlled Vowel *or* /ôr/ 57

r-Controlled Vowels *er, ir, ur* /ûr/ 59

    Suffixes *-er, -or* 63

r-Controlled Vowels *are, air, ear* /âr/ 65

Complex Vowels

Long *oo* /o͞o/ and Short *oo* /o͝o/ 67

au, aw /ô/ 70

Diphthongs *oi, oy* /oi/ 72

Diphthongs *ou, ow* /ou/ 74

Schwa 77

Silent-Letter Teams 81

Contractions 84

Suffixes

Adding Suffixes (with no change to the base word) 85

Three Spelling Rules for Adding Suffixes

Suffix Spelling Rule #1: Drop *e* 86

Suffix Spelling Rule #2: Double the Final Consonant 91

Suffix Spelling Rule #3: Change *y* to *i* 94

Homophones 97

Syllabication

Open Syllables 99

V/CV Words 100

VC/V Words 104

Consonant + *le* Syllables 106

V/V Division Pattern 111

Games

Road Race 112

Star Words 117

Pizza Spinner Game 119

Four Block 122

Fluency Voices 124

Build-a-Contraction 126

Three Blooming Spelling Rules Games 129

Suffix Spelling Rule #1: Drop the *e* 129

Suffix Spelling Rule #2: Double the Final Consonant 136

Suffix Spelling Rule #3: Change *y* to *i* 139

Syllable Sandwiches 142

INTRODUCTION

"Teaching reading is rocket science."
–Louisa Moats, Ed.D.

To teach children how to read requires a deep understanding of language and linguistics. Our brains are hardwired to speak and listen, but not to read or spell.

As teachers, reading specialists, literacy consultants, and Orton-Gillingham trainers, we have used various programs and methodologies that teach reading. We recognized the need for resources to help teachers teach foundational skills in reading and writing. We wanted to create an easy-to-use, comprehensive resource that supports structured literacy instruction based on the science of reading.

The Ultimate Book of Phonics Word Lists for Grades 1–2 contains lists of words, phrases, and sentences that feature the phonetic patterns and spelling generalizations children need to learn how to read. We've also included descriptions and explanations of various phonetic patterns to support decoding and encoding instruction.

This resource can be used in a variety of settings—across the three tiers of instruction, in general education and special education programs, and for homeschooled children. It should be noted, however, that this is a resource, not a curriculum.

How to Use the Lists, Lames, and Assessments

The lists in *The Ultimate Book of Phonics Word Lists for Grades 1–2* are organized by phonetic patterns/skills and build from words to phrases to sentences. We chose words, phrases, and sentences that are high utility and support the development of children's vocabulary.

Although the skills covered in this book are generally taught in the primary grades, many students struggle with reading and spelling acquisition well beyond second grade. For that reason, we've expanded this resource. While most of the words in the lists are basic-level words, you'll notice some of the words are in shaded boxes and some are in **boldface**. The words in shaded boxes are multisyllabic words that contain the same phonetic patterns, while the ones in boldface type are higher-level vocabulary that can be used with older students who are still in need of basic instruction. It is important to acknowledge that some students need basic reading instruction long past the early elementary years. We recognized that need and created a flexible, teacher/parent-friendly resource. A teacher, specialist, or tutor can identify the words that will best serve a child, group of students, or class.

DECODING ENGLISH

There are 26 letters in the English alphabet. These vowels and consonants come together in varying orders and combinations to form words. Children need to recognize these letters or combinations of letters in isolation and practice reading and spelling them in many words. There are 44 *phonemes* (the smallest unit of sound) that are represented by *graphemes* (letters or clusters of letters), and 72 *phonograms* (letters or series of letters that represent sounds or syllables). Some letters or combinations of letters have multiple pronunciations for reading, and some sounds have multiple spelling choices. For example, the long-*a* sound has many different spellings, including *a_e (bake), ai (rain), ay (day), eigh (neigh), ei (rein), ey (hey),* and *ea (great).* Knowing when to use these spellings for decoding and for encoding is key to reading success. Children develop a discerning eye and ear. They become linguists themselves with this kind of deep word study.

WORD LISTS FOR READING

Choose the number of words for children to read based on each child's ability. Be careful not to overload them.

You can present the words to children by writing them in columns, a grid, or on cards that can be stored for future use. Children can read up and down a column or across rows in a grid. If children's first pass at reading the words is not automatic, have them read the words again to help improve fluency. You may need to model the proper pronunciation or assist with supporting strategies for decoding.

Whether using lists or cards, note how children are reading the words: correctly or correctly with automaticity. Also, take note of student errors so you can provide guided correction and plan accordingly. In a future lesson, revisit those words for children to reread. Continue to provide other words with a similar phonetic pattern for further practice until the child no longer needs the review.

As an option, consider displaying the words in a pocket chart. After children have read through the words, ask questions or use prompts to enhance vocabulary. For example:

- *What word means . . . ?*
- *What word is the opposite of . . . ?*
- *Find a synonym for . . .*
- *Use a word in a sentence.*
- *Use two words in the same sentence.*

For a cumulative review, include words from previously taught patterns to create a mixed list. Additionally, plug the words into the game board templates to supplement single-word reading.

WORD LISTS FOR SPELLING

To build children's spelling skills, dictate words with the same phonetic pattern used in your reading lists. Include review words and words that children had trouble reading.

The number of words you dictate for spelling will depend on the child and may be fewer than the words provided for reading. Choose spelling words that are different from the words children have read but still follow the same pattern or skill. Create a master list of reading and spelling words so you can record errors for an individual child or a small group.

When you dictate a word for children to spell, it may be helpful to have them repeat or whisper the word prior to writing it to engage the auditory track. This helps enhance learning.

Collect children's spelling lists and use an error analysis diagnostically. For instance, a child who spells *bed* as *bid, red* as *rid,* or *bit* as *bet* is confusing short *e* and short *i* and needs more

The Ultimate Book of Phonics Word Lists for Grades 1–2 © by Laurie J. Cousseau and Rhonda Graff, Scholastic Inc.

practice. By looking at the errors children make, you can note areas of confusion and plan instruction accordingly.

Invite children to read back the spelling words as another pass at fluency.

When children learn the phonetic patterns and generalizations, they no longer need to study words for a weekly spelling test. They can apply their knowledge and spell many words correctly without prior studying because of the depth of their understanding.

PHRASES AND SENTENCES FOR READING

Following each word list is a phrase and sentence list for each phonetic pattern. Use these to promote oral reading fluency and to help children see how to use the words in context. The sentences can be "scooped" for phrasing.

Encourage children to read the sentences several times with increasing prosody. Feel free to modify or extend the sentences based on children's needs. You can expand the sentences orally so children are not limited by spelling. For example, you may wish to expand the sentence, "The pans and pots banged and clanged," to "The pans and pots banged and clanged when we put them back on the shelf."

PHRASES AND SENTENCES FOR DICTATION

You can also dictate the phrases and sentences. Begin with a phrase or two, then dictate sentences in increasing length. Have children repeat the phrase or sentence prior to writing it on paper.

If children struggle to remember the sentence, have them repeat it a few times prior to writing it. Encourage them to cluster phrases and clauses and to visualize the sentence.

Teach children the importance of rereading their work to check for accuracy by using the acronym CHOPS. Have children reread the sentence they wrote and check off each letter to see whether their sentence is accurate. Does it have capital letters where needed? Is it neatly written? Does it include all the words in the correct order? Is it correctly punctuated? Is every word correctly spelled? (A teacher may need to check the spelling.) This is a great way to reinforce important aspects of writing sentences.

> C – capitalization
> H – handwriting
> O – order of words
> P – punctuation
> S – spelling

Afterwards, have children read back their sentences for more practice with fluency.

VOCABULARY

An enriched vocabulary can improve understanding. The Simple View of Reading formula shows that reading comprehension is the product of strong decoding and strong language comprehension (Gough & Tunmer, 1986; Hoover & Gough, 1990).

Use the word lists to create vocabulary cards that can be used for review. You can find a template online. (See page 8 for more information on how to access the supplemental online resources.) Revisiting the words on multiple occasions in various ways helps children incorporate the words into their vocabularies.

Explore words in depth with children, helping them understand how to use the words in sentences. Note synonyms and antonyms. There are many opportunities for vocabulary exploration using the word, phrase, and sentence lists as a springboard.

GAMES

Included in this resource are 10 reproducible word games and activities that provide fun ways to reinforce the phonetic patterns and skills. Customize the blank game boards to highlight any pattern or skill. Since all the games and activities require children to read words, we recommend that an adult be present to check for accuracy.

Use guided questioning to help children understand why they made a mistake and to help them fix it. Encourage children to explain the strategies, rules, and patterns they are using. For example, *Why is that vowel long? Why would you use* ai *instead of* ay? Children develop a deeper understanding when they can explain why.

Make extra copies of each game to send home for practice and reinforcement.

ASSESSMENTS

Online, you will find informal progress-monitoring assessments for most of the skill levels in the book. Assessments for word reading, phrase reading, sentence reading, and spelling are included.

We also provide teacher record sheets to support good recordkeeping and anecdotal note-taking. Each teacher record sheet has space allocated for two different assessments— a pre- and post-test.

We have also included blank assessments and blank teacher record sheets along with detailed instructions for teachers and parents to customize their own assessments.

SUPPLEMENTAL ONLINE MATERIALS

In addition to the assessments, we also provide lists of function words, content words, and irregular words, and other useful resources online. To access these materials, go to **www.scholastic.com/phonicswordlists** and enter the password **SC766601**.

We hope you enjoy using this resource as much as we enjoyed creating it!

Glossary of Phonetic Terms

TERM	DEFINITION	EXAMPLE
Affix	A morpheme that can be added to the beginning or end of a word—a prefix or suffix	**re**visit**ed**
Breve	A symbol used to code a short-vowel sound	˘
Closed Syllable	A syllable with a single vowel closed in by a consonant or consonants; the vowel sound is short.	map, mask hen, help pin, pick cot, cloth rub, rush
Consonant	A speech sound partially blocked by teeth, lips, and/or tongue; these are classified as voiced, unvoiced, continuant, or stopped.	*b, c, d, f, g, h, j, k, l, m, n, p, q, r, s, t, v, w, x, z*
Consonant Blend Cluster	Two or more consecutive consonants that maintain their individual sounds but are coarticulated	**sk**ip **fr**og **cl**am be**nd**
Consonant Digraph	Two consonants that have one sound; these often contain the letter *h*.	*ch, sh, th, wh, ph*
Content Words	Words that have a clear semantic meaning in a sentence	The **red fox ran quickly**.
Continuant Sound	A consonant sound that can be held	"mmmmmmmmm" "sssssssssssssssssssss"
Controlled Words	Words that a child can decode based on a specific continuum of skills already taught	If a child just learned short vowels and closed syllables, a sentence with controlled words should only include words with skills taught to date and not words with long vowels or more advanced syllable types.
Decodable Words	Words that can be sounded out and contain predictable phonetic patterns	e.g., V-*e* *fame, time, home, theme, fume*
Decoding	Sounding out a word and blending to say the whole word	<u>m</u><u>ar</u><u>ch</u> • • •
Encoding	Spelling and the ability to write a word based upon the speech sounds	Spoken word: s/k/oo/l Written word: *school*
Function Word	A word whose meaning is based upon the grammatical or structural relationship with the other words in a sentence	Often linking verbs She **is** a dancer.
Grapheme	A letter or letter combination that represents a single phoneme; could be two or more letters	*sh*, as in *wish* *igh*, as in *night*
Irregular Word	A word that is not decodable because it contains uncommon sound-symbol correspondences and is not spelled the way it sounds	s**ai**d

The Ultimate Book of Phonics Word Lists for Grades 1–2 © by Laurie J. Cousseau and Rhonca Graff, Scholastic Inc.

TERM	DEFINITION	EXAMPLE
Long Vowel	A vowel that says its name; long *u* says /ū/ and /o͞o/	bake, stay me, wheel lime, sky hole, toast few, mule
Macron	A symbol used to code a long-vowel sound	–
Morpheme	The smallest unit of meaning that includes prefixes, roots, and suffixes	in vis ible
Multisyllabic Words	Words that contain more than one syllable	fan/tas/tic (3 vowels = 3 syllables)
Open Syllable	A syllable that ends with a single vowel, which has a long sound	h**e** h**i** n**o** fl**u** pa**/**per m**o**/ment
Orthographic Mapping	The mental process of forming letter-sound connections to secure the spellings, pronunciations, and meanings resulting in automatic sight recognition of a word	
Phoneme	Smallest unit of sound in spoken language; there are 44 phonemes represented by 72 written phonograms.	w/ay 2 phonemes ch/e/ck 3 phonemes
Prefix	A morpheme that comes before a base word or root that modifies its meaning	**re**turn **pre**dict **un**happy
Schwa	Although there isn't a specific letter to represent schwa, it is a vowel that often sounds like a short *u* or short *i*; it is found in an unstressed syllable; the symbol for schwa is ə.	**a**way pil**o**t jack**e**t
Scope and Sequence	A logical ordering of phonetic skills and spelling generalizations	
Short Vowel	A vowel sound that is not obstructed in a closed syllable	s**i**t j**u**mp sp**e**nd
Sight Word	A word that is recognized immediately; these may be regular or irregular.	said (irregular) say (temporarily irregular)
Stop Sound	A consonant sound that is stopped by the airstream and cannot be held	/b/, /p/, /d/, /t/
Syllable	A word or part of a word with a spoken vowel sound	
Syllable Types	There are reliably six syllable types where the pattern denotes the vowel sound.	closed (*not*) open (*no*) V-*e* (*note*) *r*-controlled (*star*) vowel team (*rain*) C-*le* (*maple*)
Suffix	A morpheme attached to the end of a base or root word that modifies the meaning or grammatical function	wind**s** wind**ed** wind**y**
Unvoiced	A consonant sound produced without vibration in the throat	/k/, /f/, /h/, /p/, /s/, /t/
Voiced	A consonant sound produced with vibration in the throat	/b/, /d/, /g/, /j/, /l/, /m/, /n/, /r/, /v/, /w/, /z/

The Ultimate Book of Phonics Word Lists for Grades 1–2 © by Laurie J. Cousseau and Rhonda Graff, Scholastic Inc.

Soft c /s/

The consonant c stands for two sounds: a hard sound /k/ and a soft sound /s/. When c is followed by the vowels e, i, or y, as in the words cent, city, or fancy, it stands for the /s/ sound. Soft c is a useful pattern to teach students of all ages. When introducing this concept to young readers, start with words that contain ce. Words with ci and cy are often multisyllabic. Teach children this mnemonic to help them remember: *Cindy went to the center wearing a fancy hat.*

Soft c Words

ace	race	embrace	**citrus**
brace	rice	except	**civic**
cent	sauce	excite	**concentrate**
chance	slice	fancy	**cycle**
choice	space	icy	**cyclone**
dance	spice	notice	**cygnet**
dice	spruce	pencil	**cypress**
face	trace	practice	**decent**
fence	twice	princess	**displace**
France	bicycle	recent	**excess**
glance	bracelet	recess	**mince**
grace	cancel	recital	**proceed**
ice	celebrate	recite	**quince**
juice	celery	science	**rancid**
lace	center	spicy	**replace**
lice	central	stencil	**replacement**
mice	cider	**accept**	sincerely
nice	circle	**access**	success
pace	circus	**cell**	thrice
place	city	**centipede**	truce
prance	concern	**cinch**	unicycle
price	December	**cite**	
prince	decide	**citizen**	

Soft c Phrases

red sauce on rice	a nice child	a sharp pencil
the last race	fancy dance	may cancel the recital
nice mice	icy juice	celery cupcakes
spicy rice	twice and thrice	celebrate in December
twice the price	icy, cold place	a long recess
trace of ice	glass of citrus juice	the fancy bracelet
nice face	glance twice	a chance to dance
a nice pencil	a decent choice	the city center
cost a cent	a circus dance	center of the circle
jump the fence twice	a rancid smell in science class	space between the fences

Soft c Sentences

Skate on the ice.	Rice is nice.
Nancy had a chance to dance.	We ate a slice of quince.
The prince wore fancy lace.	They had to cancel the recital.
Place the lace on the table.	Bruce sat under the spruce.
Cedric jumped over the fence twice.	She loves to prance and dance.
Grace will go to the dance.	Nancy has a fancy dress.
Make space for the bicycle, please.	She gave her mom a nice embrace.
The mice hid in the small space.	There was no trace of ice left.
Nancy spent just a cent.	Jace had a slice of cake.
Do celery cupcakes taste nice?	The cupcake has spices in it.
Take a chance in the race.	The fancy pony can prance.

The Ultimate Book of Phonics Word Lists for Grades 1–2 © by Laurie J. Cousseau and Rhonda Graff, Scholastic Inc.

Soft c Sentences *continued*	
I will run in the race.	The kids sing the song twice.
Her face has a nice smile.	The recent circus was a success.
Do you like spicy red sauce on rice?	The race went through the center of the city.
Would you like citrus juice or apple cider?	We need to replace the broken fence.
She sold the fancy bracelet for twice its price.	If I dance out in space, will I float?
The clown rode her unicycle at the circus.	Getting rid of recess is not a good choice.
Celia wore a fancy dress to the dance.	Trace the circle using the pencil and stencil.

Spelling Patterns *ss* vs. *ce*

When there is an /s/ sound at the end of a one-syllable word, it is never spelled with a single *s*. For example, words like *has* and *was* that end with a single *s* have a /z/ sound. Common spelling choices include:

- *-ss*, following a short vowel, as in *pass*
- *-ce*, following a long vowel in a V-*e* syllable, as *pace*
- *-se*, which is also a choice for words that originate from Old English. These words end with an *e* to prevent the singular word ending in -*s* to appear plural.

Children can contrast words ending in -*ss* with words ending in -*ce*, as in *pass* vs. *pace*.

-ss	-ce
grass	grace
lass	lace
mass	mace
miss	mice
pass	pace

Soft g /j/

The consonant g has two sounds: a hard sound /g/ and a soft sound /j/. When g is followed by the vowels e, i, or y, as in the words gem, ginger, or gym, it stands for the /j/ sound. However, this pattern is not as reliable as the soft c pattern (page 11) because in some words, such as get or gear, the g is hard. When introducing this concept to younger readers, start with the common word ending -ge. Words with gi and gy are often multisyllabic. Teach children this mnemonic to help them remember: *The magic gem turned the gym into a forest.*

Soft g Words

age	gerbil	apologize	hinge
cage	giant	apology	legend
change	gigantic	barge	logic
charge	ginger	biology	margin
gem	giraffe	congested	merge
germ	gymnast	cringe	origin
gym	gymnastics	digest	original
huge	legend	dingy	oxygen
large	magic	ecology	plunge
page	magical	engineer	rigid
range	messenger	forge	stingy
stage	stranger	fragile	suggest
strange	vegetable	fringe	tragic
emergency	agent	generation	urgent
energy	agile	giblets	verge
gentle	allergic	gist	wage

Soft g Phrases

on stage	can digest the meal	congested nose
huge gem	gerbil's cage	margin on the page
a strange noise	hard-to-digest giblets	barged into the room
on the verge	magic tricks	allergic to ginger
cold plunge	a huge smile	dingy gym
gentle breeze	fragile page	agile gymnast
gentle giants	strange tale	a note on the page
in the large room	giraffe's long neck	old age
on the next page	time to digest	lots of energy
a hot pot on the range	on the large stage	in the dingy basement

Soft g Sentences

Sit on the large stage.	At what age can you drive?
Place a note on the page.	The stage is next to the gym.
Turn the page.	Paige will plunge into icy water.
The fancy gem was huge and shiny.	The snake is in a large cage.
The play took place on a large stage.	There is a huge bump on her leg.
The ring had a huge gem on it.	The large pot was on the stove.
Make a huge change.	We will hike the huge hill.
We will watch the magic show on stage.	Change the water in the gerbil's cage.

Soft g Sentences continued	
At what age did you start to swim?	The grumpy stranger apologized.
The kids took charge of the stage.	Gerald is allergic to ginger and giblets.
The gentle breeze began to change.	The magic trick turned the gerbil into a giant.
The gentle giants were kind and friendly.	The engineer fixed the door hinge.
The pages of the old book are fragile.	I heard a strange tale about a magical place.
Turn the page to find out about magic.	The agile gymnast will flip off the stage.
The gerbil's cage was quite large.	The stranger said he grows giant vegetables.
The crazy gerbils charged into the cage.	Trees give off large amounts of oxygen.
Did you hear a strange noise from the dingy basement?	Gigantic giraffes can reach the high branches.
It can be hard to digest chicken giblets.	The gerbils in the cage have lots of energy.

The Ultimate Book of Phonics Word Lists for Grades 1–2 © by Laurie J. Cousseau and Rhonda Graff, Scholastic Inc.

/j/ Spelled -*dge*

The most common spelling for the /j/ sound is the letter *j*, which typically appears at the beginning of a word, as in *jump* and *jet*. The /j/ sound is also represented by the letter *g* when it is followed by an *e, i,* or *y,* as in *giraffe* (see Soft *g*, page 14).

The /j/ sound is commonly spelled -*dge* at the end of a one-syllable word immediately following a short vowel, as in *bridge*.

Another spelling for the /j/ sound is -*ge*. In the word *page*, for example, the spelling -*ge* follows a long vowel. This spelling can also be used after an *r*-controlled vowel, as in *forge*, or the letter *n*, as in *hinge*.

-*dge* Words

badge	hedge	ridge	**dislodge**
bridge	judge	smudge	**hodgepodge**
budge	large	wedge	**sledge**
dodge	ledge	badger	**sledgehammer**
edge	lodge	drawbridge	**sludge**
fudge	nudge	hedgehog	**smidge**
grudge	pledge	partridge	**trudge**

-*dge* Phrases

wedge of fudge	smidge of fudge	large lodge
hold a grudge	huge bridge	to make a pledge
long ridge	edge of the bridge	at the lodge
rock ledge	prickly hedge	a wedge of cheese
hot fudge on ice cream	trudge along the edge	trudge through sludge
bridge next to the lodge	a partridge and badger	hedgehog with a grudge

-dge Sentences

The judge was fair.	Eat the yummy fudge.
Lucy stayed in a lodge.	Cross the bridge over the river.
Do not hold a grudge.	Midge can hold a grudge.
I will have a smidge of fudge.	Sit on the edge of the ledge.
Take the fudge from the box.	Cut a wedge of cake.
Liz will trim the hedge.	The judge has a large desk.
I pledge to do my best.	The girl got a badge.
The long ridge goes past the edge.	I don't like to trudge through sludge.
Dodge the ball during the fast game.	There is only a smidge of fudge left.
The pup sat on the edge of the bench.	The pencil made a smudge on the paper.
Bridget ate the yummy wedge of fudge.	The prickly hedge is next to the lodge.
The rock ledge was next to the bridge.	The hedgehog and badger play jazz on stage.
We looked over the edge of the ledge.	A partridge stood on the drawbridge.
I love hot fudge on ice cream, don't you?	The hedgehog and badger are best friends.
Blake got a badge for making a pledge.	Don't upset that hedgehog with a grudge!
They used a sledgehammer to flatten the rock.	A hodgepodge of sweets is on the plate.

The Ultimate Book of Phonics Word Lists for Grades 1–2 © by Laurie J. Cousseau and Rhonda Graff, Scholastic Inc.

y Pronounced /ī/

The letter *y* acts as a consonant at the beginning of a word, as in the word *yes*. If *y* appears anywhere else in a word, however, it is considered a vowel and represents various sounds.

At the end of a one-syllable word, *y* represents the long-*i* sound /ī/, as in the word *my*. In a two-syllable word of Latin or Greek origin, such as *reply* or *typhoon*, the letter *y* in the open syllable (syllable that ends in a vowel) is pronounced with the long-*i* sound, /ī/.

y Pronounced /ī/ Words

by	pry	cycle	**hyphen**
cry	shy	deny	**imply**
dry	sky	reply	**occupy**
fly	sly	retry	**spry**
fry	spy	supply	**sty**
my	try	**ally**	typhoon
ply	why	**defy**	**wry**

y Pronounced /ī/ Phrases

a shy spy	my dog	spy with one eye
a spry spy	a sly fox	pink sky
sly spy	pry the lid	in the big sky
shy fly	why, oh, why	dark sky
black fly	my, oh, my	try to fly
fast fly	by and by	wry face
my fly	try and try	dry eye
my bag	two-ply	try harder
will dry up	by the pond	why cry

y Pronounced /ī/ Sentences

Fly fast, small fly.	The fly is up in the sky.
The sly spy hid by the bush.	My shy dog loves to lick my hand.
The fast fly flew by with a buzz.	Pry the lid off the big box.
A black fly is stuck in the web.	I have a sty in my eye.
Why, oh, why is the sky so black?	Jess made a wry face at the joke.
The fly stayed dry even in the rain.	My, oh, my, did you see the pink sky?
The shy boy began to cry.	Let's have a fish fry for lunch.
The fly can try to land on the ledge.	Try to fly up into the sky.
The two-ply tissue paper feels soft.	There was not a dry eye after the show ended.
The sly fox will run past by and by.	Can you find the spy with one eye?

y Pronounced /ĭ/

In the middle of a closed syllable (syllable that ends in a consonant), the letter *y* has a short /ĭ/ sound, as in the word *myth*. These words are often Greek in origin and are best introduced to upper elementary and older students as the vocabulary is more sophisticated.

gym	gymnast	syrup	**oxygen**
lynx	lyric	**cryptic**	**rhythm**
myth	mystery	**cygnet**	**symptom**
crystal	Olympics	**gypsy**	**system**
cymbals	symbol	**hymn**	**typical**

The Ultimate Book of Phonics Word Lists for Grades 1–2 © by Laurie J. Cousseau and Rhonda Graff. Scholastic Inc.

y Pronounced /ē/

The letter *y* acts as a consonant at the beginning of a word, as in the word *yes*. If *y* appears anywhere else in a word, however, it is considered a vowel that represents various sounds.

The letter *y* at the end of a multisyllable word can represent the long-*e* sound /ē/, as in *baby* or *candy*. A mnemonic, such as *my candy*, can help anchor these two pronunciations of the letter *y* (long *i* and long *e*).

y Pronounced /ē/ Words

baby	empty	many	spicy
beauty	entry	merry	story
belly	fairy	mommy	sunny
berry	family	mummy	tasty
body	fancy	navy	tidy
bunny	funny	only	tiny
candy	granny	party	ugly
carry	gravy	penny	**dainty**
city	handy	plenty	**envy**
copy	happy	pony	**factory**
county	hobby	pretty	**hazy**
cozy	holly	puppy	**ivy**
crazy	jelly	ruby	**musty**
daddy	jolly	shady	**petty**
dairy	juicy	shiny	**puny**
daisy	kitty	silly	**taffy**
dizzy	lacy	sixty	**tardy**
duty	lady	smoky	**vacancy**
easy	lobby	soggy	**wily**

Suffix -y

The letter *y* (pronounced /ē/) can be attached to an unchanging base word and act as a suffix, as in *bumpy* and *messy*. Adding the suffix -*y* changes the meaning of the word and turns it into an adjective that can mean "characterized by" or "full of." One way to introduce -*y* as a suffix is to brainstorm weather words, such as *windy*, *rainy*, and *stormy*.

bossy	foamy	lumpy	rocky	stormy
bumpy	fuzzy	messy	rusty	sudsy
chewy	goofy	mighty	salty	sulky
chilly	grainy	minty	sandy	thirsty
crispy	grassy	misty	sleepy	tricky
crunchy	grouchy	moody	smelly	wacky
curly	grumpy	mossy	snowy	windy
dirty	handy	mushy	soapy	woody
dusty	itchy	oily	sporty	
fluffy	lucky	rainy	sticky	

y Pronounced /ē/ Phrases

sweet baby	fuzzy cloth	soapy suds
happy and silly	chilly drink	tiny and tidy
cost a penny	bumpy and lumpy	sticky jelly
plenty of candy	silly puppy	itchy skin
tiny pony	sleepy kitty	windy and stormy
chewy bone	sleepy and grumpy	cozy blanket
mossy hill	shady tree	shiny button
juicy fruit	spicy dish	lacy scarf
rocky and grassy path	misty morning	messy room
rainy sky	tasty fish fry	hazy sky

The Ultimate Book of Phonics Word Lists for Grades 1–2 © by Laurie J. Cousseau and Rhonda Graff. Scholastic Inc

y Pronounced /ē/ Sentences

Plenty of candy costs a penny.	His bedroom is tiny and tidy.
The food was mushy and salty.	The plate is full of sticky jelly.
The silly puppy ate the chewy bone.	The sandwich is bumpy and lumpy.
Soapy suds are in the sink.	The night is windy and stormy.
That joke is so funny and silly.	I had tasty, crispy fish for lunch.
His skin looks itchy and bumpy.	Her dress is made of fuzzy cloth.
The fairy tale tells the story of a tiny pony.	That joke made me feel happy and silly.
My empty belly made me feel grumpy.	The shady tree is great when it is sunny.
It is nice to have a chilly drink on a hot day.	The cozy blanket keeps me warm at night.

Mixed /ī/ and /ē/ Sentences

The rainy sky got stormy.	Fanny told the story of the sly fox.
The spy with the curly hair is shy.	The fly made my skin itchy.
The shy spy has a navy cap.	Try to catch a fly on a windy day.
Try to sip a chilly drink.	Why did the fluffy puppy run by?
The sky is hazy and smoky.	What if candy fell from the sky?
Oh my, the silly fly got lost in the sky.	The shy puppy hid under a shady tree.
The spy solved the case of the missing fly.	The crazy fly buzzed around my eye.

In a two-syllable word ending in *y*, the middle consonant may sometimes need to be doubled. This protects the short vowel in the first syllable. For instance, in the word *hobby*, the *b* is doubled to keep the *o* in the first syllable closed in and short. If there was only one *b*, the word would be pronounced /hō bē/. The first syllable would be open, and its vowel would be long.

Suffix -*ly*

When the suffix -*ly* is added to the end of a word, the word often becomes an adverb that answers the question "how." The adverb commonly modifies a verb or adjective, as in "spoke quickly."

Suffix -*ly* Words

badly	lastly	stiffly	silently
blankly	lately	strangely	sincerely
blindly	lively	strongly	suddenly
boldly	lonely	sweetly	usually
bravely	loosely	thinly	**annually**
briefly	loudly	tightly	**bluntly**
clearly	madly	weekly	**brashly**
closely	monthly	widely	**earnestly**
costly	mostly	wildly	**flatly**
crisply	nicely	wisely	**gingerly**
darkly	proudly	carefully	**overly**
finely	quickly	evenly	**promptly**
firmly	rarely	extremely	**remotely**
freely	rudely	finally	**scarcely**
gladly	sadly	openly	**sharply**
hardly	slowly	politely	**shrewdly**
hopefully	smoothly	quietly	**smugly**
kindly	softly	recently	**tautly**

The Ultimate Book of Phonics Word Lists for Grades 1–2 © by Laurie J. Caruccio and Rhonda Graff, Scholastic Inc.

Suffix -ly Phrases

walked slowly	quietly nudged	thinly covered
bravely followed	stomped loudly	wildly danced
finely chopped	suddenly arrived	briefly stated
evenly placed	tightly pulled	loosely woven
quietly entered	politely responded	nicely done
slowly turned	smiled sweetly	politely asked
gladly helped	spoke kindly	spoke freely
strongly refused	slowly stretched	stood stiffly

Suffix -ly Sentences

Sadly, we lost the game.	The girls proudly sang their song.
The carrots were finely chopped.	Cole stood stiffly with his cast on.
Holly bravely followed her dad.	They carefully lifted the big box.
We quietly entered the room slowly.	The kids' posters were nicely done.
The stones were evenly placed.	They danced wildly in the park.
The cloth was loosely woven.	Your concert was nicely done.
They suddenly arrived at our home.	Sandy smiled sweetly at her friends.
Eve turned slowly to find a surprise!	Paul politely asked to have a turn.
The monster stomped loudly in the cave.	Pat and Pete walked slowly up the path.
We bravely went into the dragon's cave.	We finally finished our weekly homework.
The balls were evenly placed in the gym.	The cat slowly stretched after waking up.

Long *a* /ā/ Spelled *ai, ay*

The vowel teams *ai* and *ay* both have a long-a sound, /ā/. Children can easily determine which spelling to use based on the position of the vowel team in the word. Typically, *ai* comes at the beginning or middle of a word, as in *aim* or *mail*. The vowel team *ay* comes at the end of a word, as in *day*. (Consider introducing the days of the week since they all end in *day*.) Teach children this mnemonic to help them retain these two spellings: *rainy day.*

Multisyllabic words that contain *ai* or *ay* are often compound words, such as *mailbox*, or a base word with a suffix added, such as *stainless*.

/ā/ Spelled *ai* Words

bait	paint	contain	remain
braid	plain	daily	strainer
brain	praise	daisy	aid
chain	rail	detail	aim
drain	rain	entertain	await
fail	raise	exclaim	claim
faint	sail	explain	dainty
gain	snail	faithful	frail
grain	sprain	mailbox	hail
jail	stain	mermaid	maintain
laid	strain	obtain	quail
maid	tail	painful	quaint
mail	trail	pigtail	raid
main	train	railroad	remainder
nail	waist	railway	Spain
paid	wait	raincoat	stainless
pail	airplane	raindrop	tailor
pain	complain	raisin	vain

/ā/ Spelled *ai* Phrases

a big stain	a bad sprain	a rocky trail
a gold chain	a white daisy	a plain bagel
frail snail	pail of nails	rain and hail
daisy chain	pail of grain	painted chain
dainty quail	remain on the train	can braid her pigtail
rain in Spain	wait for the mail	stain at his waist
wet paint	quaint quail	painted raincoat
contain raisins	paid to work	snail trail
main trail	had to wait in vain	painful sprain

/ā/ Spelled *ai* Sentences

The dog chased its tail.	Get the mail from the mailbox.
Simon will sail on the sea.	Clean the stain on your shirt.
The snail left no trail.	The chain fell off the bike.
Dana made a long daisy chain.	It began to rain and hail.
The pail of nails is on the porch.	We waited in vain for the train.
I have a sprain in my ankle.	The rain and the hail lasted for hours.
The dainty quail twitched her tail.	Henry fed the horse a pail of grain.
The pail of nails is very rusty.	Remain in the train at the next stop.
The pail of grain needs to be dry.	Mom has bait to help catch a fish.
The tale of the dog with no tail is long!	Jane will ride the train to Spain.
I got a painful sprain on the winding trail.	Would you like to sail or ride on a train?
The painted chain got rusty in the rain.	The long braids in her hair were lovely.

/ā/ Spelled *ay* Words

bay	spray	Friday	Thursday
clay	stay	layer	today
day	stray	maybe	Tuesday
gay	sway	Monday	Wednesday
gray	tray	okay	yesterday
hay	way	pathway	**bray**
jay	always	payment	**decay**
lay	away	player	**dismay**
may	birthday	railway	**display**
pay	crayon	runway	**fray**
play	daytime	Saturday	**hayloft**
pray	driveway	subway	**nay**
ray	hallway	Sunday	**portray**
say	haystack		

/ā/ Spelled *ay* Phrases

kids play	can stay longer	can pay with cash
dry hay	long day	wet spray
tray of clay	wax crayons	gray day
a stray pup	a long driveway	will stay longer
stay and sway	loud blue jay	donkey's bray
play day	birthday in May	maybe today

/ā/ Spelled *ay* Sentences

Ray will jump in the hay.	Put the hay in the barn.
The stray puppy hid by the bay.	Please stay to play.
The donkey's bray was quite loud.	There was no sun on the gray day.
The tray of clay is on the table.	May day is a time for playing.
Let's stay longer to play.	Monday was a very gray day.
I will pay for the clay.	Troy's birthday is on Tuesday.
Let us sit and rest by the bay.	You can say okay or maybe.
The loud blue jay stayed at the feeder.	Maybe today will be the day to play.
There is a way to sharpen wax crayons.	The stray puppy is going to stay with us.
We wanted to stay and sway to the music.	Jay's birthday is on the first Sunday in May.

Mixed *ai* and *ay* Sentences

Let's sail away to Spain.	It may rain in May.
Stay on the long train.	The hay is in the pail.
Say you will stay and paint with me.	Please stay and play with the quail.
The blue jay flew away in the rain.	The stray snail found its way.
The mail may get here today.	Len lay down on the long trail.
It is better to feed horses hay than grain.	Maybe we can take the train to Spain.

Homophones Spelled *a_e* vs. *ai*

When you introduce long-vowel spelling combinations, children become exposed to *homophones*—words that sound the same but are spelled differently and have different meanings. Children often learn which spelling option to choose after multiple exposures reading and spelling these words in context. (See page 97 for more homophones.)

a_e	ai
pale	pail
made	maid
pane	pain
tale	tail

Long *a* /ā/ Spelled *eigh, ei, ey, ea*

In addition to *ai* and *ay*, the long-*a* sound can also be spelled with *a*, as in *lady*, and *a_e*, as in *lake*. Less common spellings include *eigh, ei, ey,* and *ea*. Teach children this mnemonic that features eight spellings for the long-*a* sound: *Lady Jane sailed the bay with her eight reindeer, who said, "Hey, this is great!"*

/ā/ Spelled *eigh, ei, ey, ea* Words

eigh			
eight	weight	eighty	**freight**
sleigh	eighteen	neighbor	**neigh**
weigh			
ei			
rein	**deign**	**heirloom**	skein
vein	**feign**	reign	veil
reindeer	**feint**		
ey			
grey	prey	**survey**	**whey**
hey	they		
ea			
break	great	steak	yea

The Ultimate Book of Phonics Word Lists for Grades 1–2 © by Laurie J. Cousseau and Rhonda Graff, Scholastic Inc.

/ā/ Spelled *eigh*, *ei*, *ey*, *ea* Phrases

eight neighbors	reindeer reins	curds and whey
weight of the sleigh	looking for prey	great steak
need a break	looks great	reindeer fly
eight-second break	freight train	weighs a lot
eighteen sleighs	blue vein	eighty-year reign
feinted to the left	skein of yarn	will survey the site

/ā/ Spelled *eigh*, *ei*, *ey*, *ea* Sentences

The reindeer's reins got loose.	The lion was hunting for its prey.
Does a reindeer neigh or bleat?	We took an eight-second break.
The vein on his arm is blue.	The queen had an eighty-year reign.
Please roll up the long skein of yarn.	We invited eight neighbors for tea.
Santa had eighteen sleighs in the barn.	She knit the veil from a skein of yarn.
The weight of the sleigh is eighty pounds.	We ate curds and whey for breakfast.
The freight weighs more than eight tons.	The steak tastes great with mashed potatoes.
The boxer feinted to the left and then to the right.	The workers will survey the site where the house will be built.

Long e /ē/ Spelled ee, ea

The most common spellings for the long-e sound, /ē/, are *ee* and *ea*. Both vowel teams may appear at the beginning of words (*eel* or *eat*) or at the end (*tree* or *sea*), but they are most often found in the middle of words.

Children need multiple exposures reading and spelling these words to help them learn which spelling to choose. Take time to discuss meaning and provide examples of usage. Sometimes providing children with a generalization helps them choose the correct spelling. For example, some words that relate to food tend to be spelled with *ea*, such as *eat, meal, peach, meat, feast, peas,* and *peanut*. Some *ea* words relating to water include *beach, stream, steam,* and *sea*.

/ē/ Spelled *ee* Words

bee	feel	peep	sleet
beef	feet	queen	sleeve
beep	free	reed	sneeze
beet	freeze	reef	speech
breeze	geese	reel	speed
cheek	green	screech	squeeze
cheep	greet	screen	steel
cheese	heel	see	steep
creek	jeep	seed	street
creep	keep	seek	sweep
deed	knee	seem	sweet
deep	kneel	seen	tee
deer	meet	seep	teen
eel	need	sheep	teeth
fee	peek	sheet	three
feed	peel	sleep	tree

The Ultimate Book of Phonics Word Lists for Grades 1–2 © by Laurie J. Cousseau and Rhonda Graff, Scholastic Inc.

/ē/ Spelled *ee* Words *continued*			
weed	fifteen	sixteen	**greed**
week	fourteen	speedy	**heed**
weep	freedom	thirteen	**keel**
wheel	indeed	weekday	**keen**
agree	kneecap	weekend	**lee**
asleep	needle	**beech**	**meek**
beehive	nineteen	**esteem**	**proceed**
beekeeper	seaweed	**feeble**	**spree**
beetle	seedling	**flee**	**steeple**
eighteen	seventeen	**fleet**	**tweeze**

/ē/ Spelled *ee* Phrases

cut the green grass	on the screen	on two feet
white teeth	a queen's throne	on the street
bees from the hive	even keel	red beets
green knees	green weeds	bike wheels
three sheep	reeds in the reef	wee teeth
meek sheep	speedy jeep	beep-beep
green weeds	deep sleep	sheep asleep
new seedling	green cheese	tiny peep
flat wheel	missing teeth	two-day weekend
geese on the pond	heel of the sock	sixteen beetles

/ē/ **Spelled** *ee* Sentences

Let's meet for lunch.	Keep the sheets on the bed.
I need to sleep.	Feed the sheep by threes.
Free the bees from the hive.	A soft breeze feels so nice.
Let's meet under the elm tree.	Keep an even keel while sailing.
Peel the red beets for lunch.	Theo lost three teeth in a week.
Sweep the street with a brush.	The reeds in the reef grew wild.
There were green weeds in the park.	The green cheese made me sneeze.
Set the bees free!	Beep-beep went the green jeep.
Three sheep drove the speedy jeep.	The green grass stained my knees.
Meet the queen in front of the throne.	Use the heels of your feet to feel the rug.
Sixteen beetles began to creep across the rug.	The wheel fell off the car in the street.
I had seen the sleet fall in sheets on the street.	Pluck the green weeds from under the trees.

/ē/ **Spelled** *ea* Words

beach	cheap	each	heap	leap
bead	cheat	east	heat	leash
beak	clean	eat	jeans	least
bean	cream	feast	lead	leave
beast	deal	flea	leaf	leaves
beat	dear	gleam	leak	meal
bleach	dream	heal	lean	mean

The Ultimate Book of Phonics Word Lists for Grades 1–2 © by Laurie J. Cousseau and Rhonda Graff, Scholastic Inc.

/ē/ Spelled *ea* Words *continued*				
meat	seal	treat	northeast	**beam**
near	seam	veal	oatmeal	**bleak**
neat	seat	weak	peacock	**breach**
pea	sneak	wheat	peanut	**feat**
peach	speak	yeast	repeat	**heave**
peak	steal	backseat	seaside	**plead**
please	steam	beneath	seaweed	**pleat**
reach	stream	daydream	sneakers	**retreat**
read	tea	drumbeat	southeast	**reveal**
real	teach	eagle	steamboat	**zeal**
scream	teal	easy	teacup	
sea	team	meanwhile	teammate	

/ē/ Spelled *ea* Phrases

out of the heat	weak tea	clean and shiny
by the stream	a pair of sneakers	heal a cut
sandy beach	heap of peas	blue jeans
ripe peaches	neat pile of leaves	hear the drumbeat
peaches and cream	clean stream	huge leap
cream of wheat	eagle's beak	seal on the beach
sunrise in the east	dog's leash	peak of the hill
by the sea	cheap seats	torn jeans
a huge feast	dream team	out of reach

/ē/ Spelled *ea* Sentences

Fish live in the sea.	Use a leash to walk the dog.
Will likes to drink weak tea.	Let's eat a peach at the beach.
Heat the meat on the stove.	We can leap across the stream.
Let's read a book in a cozy chair.	Your room is as neat as a pin.
We can help clean the sandy beach.	The eagle flew east for a feast.
Sal dreams about the seaside.	The stream is quite clean.
I like to eat ripe peaches with cream.	The dream team ran out of steam.
I like to read about eagles being free.	It took us a while to reach the sea.
We had peas at the cheap feast.	Bella loves to wear blue jeans.
Jean likes cream of wheat for breakfast.	The dog ran along the beach without his leash.
Sometimes I dream about the stories I read.	He made a huge leap into the leaf pile.
The dog's leash was just out of reach.	There were seals playing near the beach.

Mixed *ee* and *ea* Sentences

Please keep the beach clean.	The eagle was seen flying east.
The peach tea tasted sweet.	Eels can live in the deep green sea.
The sheep began to leap and bleat.	Please peel the beets and peaches.
The sleek seals played in the sea.	My jeans were torn at the knee.
She had sweet dreams about seals.	Take a peek at the mountain peak.
The wheels on the jeep are weak.	Let's meet up to have a feast.

The Ultimate Book of Phonics Word Lists for Grades 1–2 © by Laurie J. Cousseau and Rhonda Graff, Scholastic Inc.

Short e /ĕ/ Spelled ea

In addition to the long-e sound, the vowel team *ea* also represents the short-e sound /ĕ/, as in *head*.

/ĕ/ Spelled *ea* Words

bread	read	breakfast	meadow
breath	spread	feather	measure
dead	sweat	headlines	pleasant
dread	thread	healthy	ready
head	threat	heaven	steady
health	wealth	heavy	sweater
lead	ahead	instead	wealthy
meant	already	leather	weather

/ĕ/ Spelled *ea* Phrases

red feather	spread on bread	read the headlines
thread the needle	steady breath	pleasant meadow
healthy and wealthy	ready to measure	sweater weather
heavy lead bar	steady pace	went ahead

/ĕ/ Spelled *ea* Sentences

She held a red feather in her hand.	We rested in the pleasant meadow.
He spread butter on his bread.	Fall is sweater weather.
Thread the needle to darn your sock.	He took a steady breath and jumped.
The heavy lead weight was at the end of the chain.	We were ahead in the race due to our steady pace.

Mixed Long *ea* and **Short *ea*** Sentences

Steam your sweater to clean it.	Use your head before you leap.
We had wheat bread for a meal.	Put the dead leaves in a neat pile.
Breathe in and take a long breath.	The healthy breakfast was cheap.
The lead weight was not very clean.	The seam on the leather pants split.
The dog on the leash was ahead of us.	Peas and peaches are healthy snacks.
I would like to have beans instead of peas.	The birds have long beaks and blue feathers.
The seals return to the sea during stormy weather.	The sweater had beads and feathers on it.
Spread the sweet cream on the bread.	The weather in the east seems pleasant.
Are you ready to read in front of the class?	We could hear the steady drum beats.
The heat made us sweat in the meadow.	Leaves and feathers floated on the stream.

The Ultimate Book of Phonics Word Lists for Grades 1–2 © by Laurie J. Cousseau and Rhonda Graff. Scholastic Inc.

Long e /ē/ Spelled ey, ie, ei

The long-e sound has many spellings in addition to y (page 21) and ee and ea (page 32). Another vowel team that represents the /ē/ sound is -ey, which comes at the end of words. Sometimes these are called "key" words, as in *donkey*, *monkey*, and *turkey*. Other /ē/ vowel teams include *ie* and *ei*. Share with students the adage, "*i* before *e* except after *c*." [It's not a very reliable rule, though, as we show in the word list below.] After a soft *c*, the spelling *ei* is commonly seen in words such as *ceiling* and *receive*.

/ē/ Spelled ey, ie, ei Words

ey			
key	jersey	turkey	jockey
chimney	journey	valley	motley
donkey	kidney	alley	parsley
hockey	money	barley	pulley
honey	monkey	curtsey	trolley
ie			
chief	shriek	cookie	fiend
field	thief	goalie	grief
fierce	achieve	movie	pierce
niece	belief	relief	siege
piece	believe	brief	wield
shield	brownie	diesel	yield
ei			
weird	neither	conceit	protein
ceiling	receipt	deceive	seize
either	receive	perceive	

/ē/ Spelled *ey, ie, ei* Phrases

missing key	curly parsley	firm belief
silly donkey	long journey	piece of pie
lively monkey	motley display	diesel fuel
barley fields	kidney pie	sneaky thief
hockey jersey	horse jockey	brief visit
strong receiver	cracked ceiling	receipt for the honey
healthy protein	weird feeling	monkey shriek

/ē/ Spelled *ey, ie, ei* Sentences

My key to the door is missing.	I have the receipt for the honey.
The curly parsley started to wilt.	Eating protein is very healthy.
The jeep uses diesel fuel.	The thief stole a piece of apple pie.
The monkey began to shriek loudly.	The curly parsley was in the salad.
The silly donkey began to bray and kick.	The market had a motley display of fruit.
I have a firm belief that we will win!	Would you like a piece of kidney pie?
The barley fields were yellow and brown.	A lively monkey came for tea and honey.
She wore her winning hockey jersey.	The sneaky thief hid behind the bush.
The horse jockey rode on a long journey.	I have a weird feeling the ceiling will crack.
A turkey and a donkey went on a journey.	Polly believes she should have a brownie.

The Ultimate Book of Phonics Word Lists for Grades 1–2 © by Laurie J. Cousseau and Rhonda Graff, Scholastic Inc.

Long *i* /ī/ Spelled *igh*

The most common spellings for the long-*i* sound are *igh* and *y* (see page 19). The spelling *igh* is sometimes called the "three-letter *i*" and is commonly followed by the letter *t*, as in *night*. As previously introduced, the letter *y* as a vowel comes at the end of a one-syllable word, as in *my*, and in an open syllable, as in *rely*.

/ī/ Spelled *igh* Words

bright	night	delight	spotlight
fight	right	flashlight	sunlight
flight	sigh	frighten	tonight
fright	sight	headlight	**blight**
high	thigh	lightning	**insight**
knight	tight	midnight	**limelight**
light	brightly	moonlight	**slight**
might	daylight		

/ī/ Spelled *igh* Phrases

in your sight	a tight spot	a deep sigh
bright light	soft moonlight	daylight hours
take flight	bright sunlight	slight bite
leap high	strike of lightning	tight squeeze
bright night-light	such a sight	after midnight
knight on a horse	mighty knight	slight turn to the right
lightning at midnight	flashlight tag	filled with delight

/ī/ Spelled *igh* Sentences

Turn on the light, so we can see.	Take a late-night flight.
The flight left on time.	The words *light* and *night* rhyme.
A bright light shone all night.	I like to read at night.
The mighty knight had a fright.	Take a slight turn to the right.
The lightning at midnight lit the sky.	Let's play flashlight tag tonight.
She began to sigh and sigh, oh my.	The spotlight lit the stage at night.
The knight on the horse sat high in the saddle.	We were filled with delight when the sunlight returned.
The birds will take flight in the morning.	We wore sunglasses in the bright sunlight.
The knight can't leap high in his armor.	We saw lightning at last night's storm.
Getting into the small car was a tight squeeze.	Tonight, we want to hike in the moonlight.
Soft white moonlight lit the night sky.	Daylight hours are longer in the summer.

Homophones With Long *i*

When you introduce long-vowel spelling combinations, children become exposed to *homophones*—words that sound the same but are spelled differently and have different meanings. Children often learn which spelling option to choose after multiple exposures reading and spelling these words in context. (See page 97 for more homophones.)

hi	high
site	sight
write	right
night	knight

The Ultimate Book of Phonics Word Lists for Grades 1–2 © by Laurie 1 Coursey and Rhonda Graff Scholastic Inc

Long *i* /ī/ Spelled *ie, y_e*

Less common spellings for /ī/ include *ie*, as in *pie*, as well as *y_e*, as in *type* and *rhyme*. Words with the *y_e* pattern are Greek in origin.

/ī/ Spelled *ie, y_e* Words

ie			
cries	fries	spies	retie
die	lie	tie	untie
dried	pie	tried	vie
flies	skies		

y_e			
rhyme	tyke	hype	pyre
style	type	lyre	thyme

/ī/ Spelled *ie, y_e* Phrases

peach pie	sweet pie	tied shoelaces
vie for the title	told a lie	retie the bow
untie the knot	striped tie	floppy tie
dress with style	stringed lyre	type a letter
a lot of hype	small tyke	rhyme and verse
spies in the skies	burning pyre	dried thyme
dried flowers	flies on my fries	blue skies
can untie the ties	wore a tie with style	thyme in the sauce

/ī/ Spelled *ie, y_e* Sentences

The peach pie was sweet.	Ruby dresses with style.
Reed untied the bow on the gift.	The tyke tried to tie his shoelaces.
Lemon thyme has a minty taste.	Troy learned to type in school.
The dried flowers are in the vase.	Yuck, there are flies on my fries!
The blue skies came after the rain.	Kyle wore a striped tie with style.
There is thyme in the sauce.	Tammy told a lie about eating the pie.
He fell because his shoelaces were untied.	A huge piece of pie landed on my tie.
The players vied for the title of Best Team.	The small tyke loves to make rhymes.
The letter was typed, not written by hand.	The movie got a lot of hype in the papers.

Long o /ō/ Spelled oa, ow

The most common spellings of the long-o sound /ō/ are oa and ow. The vowel team oa can appear at the beginning of a word, as in oak, or in the middle, as in boat. The spelling ow often appears at the end of a word, as in grow.

/ō/ Spelled oa Words

boat	groan	soak	roadblock
cloak	load	soap	roadshow
coach	loaf	throat	soapsuds
coal	loan	toad	tugboat
coast	moan	toast	unload
coat	moat	whoa	**boast**
croak	oak	coastline	**charcoal**
float	oats	cockroach	**coax**
foal	roach	oatmeal	**crossroad**
foam	road	overload	**gloat**
goal	roam	railroad	**oath**
goat	roast	raincoat	**poach**

/ō/ Spelled oa Phrases

soap on a dish	toad on the boat	feed the goats
goat on the road	moan and groan	crunchy toast
hungry goat	foamy soap	roasted oats
tiny blue boat	cross the moat	float and soak
along the coast	spotted toad	baby foal

The Ultimate Book of Phonics Word Lists for Grades 1–2 © by Laurie J. Cousseau and Rhonda Graff, Scholastic Inc.

/ō/ Spelled *oa* Phrases *continued*		
will drive on the road	strong tugboat	wet raincoat
big old oak tree	long cloak	made a goal
floating boat	loaf of bread	roamed far and wide

/ō/ Spelled *oa* Sentences

Hang your coat on the hook.	The roast is in the oven.
The truck picked up the load.	The toad rested on the boat.
Oak trees love to soak up the sun.	The lone toad croaked loudly.
The sad little boat can't float.	Toast got stuck in my throat.
Let's roam along the coast.	Soak the dusty coat in soapy suds.
She made the winning goal.	Float in the lake and soak up the sun.
The toad ate the whole loaf of bread.	Coach helped the team score five goals!
The goat made an oath to cross the moat.	Three hungry goats ate crunchy toast.
The foal slept under the shady oak tree.	A tiny blue boat floats along the coast.
The heavy load made him moan and groan.	A spotted toad went across the road.

The Ultimate Book of Phonics Word Lists for Grades 1–2 © by Laurie J. Cousseau and Rhonda Graff. Scholastic Inc.

/ō/ Spelled *ow* Words

blow	own	fishbowl	snowflake
bow	row	follow	snowman
bowl	show	grown-up	sparrow
crow	shown	hollow	swallow
flow	slow	pillow	willow
flown	snow	pillowcase	window
glow	sow	rainbow	yellow
grow	throw	roadshow	**mellow**
grown	thrown	rowboat	**minnow**
growth	tow	shadow	**overthrow**
know	arrow	slowly	**shallow**
known	below	snowball	**showy**
low	elbow	snowfall	**stow**
mow	fellow		

/ō/ Spelled *ow* Phrases

soft pillow	low branch	open window
steady flow	slow snowfall	bent elbow
bow and arrow	fluffy snow	minnow in the fishbowl
mellow crow	golden glow	long shadow
bowl of fruit	grown so tall	will mow the grass
can row the boat	will sow the seeds	can throw the ball
hollow tube	rainbow in the sky	a nice fellow

/ō/ Spelled *ow* Sentences

The mellow crow sang low and slow.	The minnow swam in the fishbowl.
The farmer will sow the seeds.	Sow the seeds and they will grow.
Trace your shadow with chalk.	Lay your head on the soft pillow.
The bowl of fruit was full.	You have grown so tall.
Do not throw the snowball at me.	Owen climbed the low willow tree.
Go slowly when you mow the grass.	The glow of the sun came in the window.

Mixed *oa* and *ow* Phrases

slow boat	bowl of oatmeal	showy cloak
yellow raincoat	below the oak	fellow with a coat
her own boat	shallow moat	traveling roadshow
slow roast	showy goat	my own foal

Mixed *oa* and *ow* Sentences

The lone crow had flown away.	Stow the coat below the boat.
I own a showy cloak that glows.	Row your boat along the coast.
The tug will tow the yellow boat.	We will row the yellow boat.
Do not throw your bowl of oats.	The snowman has two eyes of coal.
The slow toad wore a yellow raincoat.	The sun cast a shadow below the oak.
Joan groaned when she banged her elbow.	We will cross the shallow moat in a rowboat.

The Ultimate Book of Phonics Word Lists for Grades 1–2 © by Laurie 1. Cousseau and Rhonda Graff, Scholastic Inc.

Long o /ō/ Spelled oe, ou

Less common vowel teams that represent the sound /ō/ include oe, as in toe, and ou, as shoulder.

/ō/ Spelled oe, ou Words

oe			
doe	Joe	tiptoe	**oboe**
hoe	toe	**foe**	**woe**
ou			
though	boulder	shoulder	

/ō/ Spelled oe, ou Phrases

gentle doe	tone of the oboe	tic-tac-toe
big toe	Joe's foe	heel to toe
large boulder	round shoulder	shoulder to toe
tiptoe quietly	woe is me	though it is small

/ō/ Spelled oe, ou Sentences

Tiptoe quietly down the stairs.	"Woe is me," said the doe.
We stretched shoulder to toe.	Though it is small, the room is cozy.
I stubbed my big toe on the hoe.	Let's play tic-tac-toe with Monroe.
Joe's foe went toe to toe with Moe.	A large boulder blocked the road.
The gentle doe eats leaves on tippy toes.	How long is your foot from heel to toe?
He hurt his shoulder picking up the boulder.	The tone of the oboe is low and slow.

Long u /ū/ and Long oo /o͞o/ Spelled ew, ue

The long-u /ū/ and the long-oo /o͞o/ sounds share a few spellings, such as open u, u_e, ew, and ue.

Keywords for long-u spellings include *music* (open u), *cute* (u_e), *few* (ew), and *rescue* (ue). The vowel team *eu* (*feud*) also stands for the long-u sound, but this spelling does not include many age-appropriate words. (Note: You can find vowel-consonant-e (VCe) lists in the Grades K–1 version of this book, while open-syllable lists are on page 99).

Keywords for long-oo spellings include *student* (open u), *tune* (u_e), *grew* (ew), and *glue* (ue). See page 52 for other spellings of the /o͞o/ sound. For the most common spelling of the /o͞o/ sound (oo), see page 67.

/ū/ Spelled ew, ue Words

ew /ū/			
ewe	fewer	hew	sinew
few	nephew	hewn	skew
mew	askew	pew	spew
ue /ū/			
fuel	argue	rescue	cue
hue	continue	value	venue

/o͞o/ Spelled ew, ue Words

ew /o͞o/			
blew	knew	jewel	newt
chew	new	newspaper	shrew
dew	news	anew	shrewd
drew	screw	brew	slew
flew	stew	crew	strewn
grew	threw	mildew	whew

ue /o͞o/			
blue	true	**accrue**	**fondue**
clue	issue	**avenue**	**gruesome**
due	statue	**bluebird**	**pursue**
glue	tissue	**ensue**	**revenue**
Sue		**flue**	

Mixed /ū/ and /o͞o/ Phrases

wooly ewe	shiny jewel	a few newts
crooked screw	the able crew	fish stew
blue hue	baby bluebird	blue statue
true clue	true value	soft tissue

Mixed /ū/ and /o͞o/ Sentences

A few birds flew away.	The crew enjoyed fish stew.
The ewe began to chew the newspaper.	My shrewd nephew knew the jewel was fake.
Drew fixed the screw that was askew.	The cat said "mew" as it licked the dew.
A few newts crossed the avenue.	Lewis cleaned the mildew off his shoe.
The glue has a blue hue.	Rescue the baby bluebird from the nest.
The blue statue stands in the avenue.	Sue found the true clue under the statue.
What is the true value of the old statue?	Pursue the blue car down the avenue.

Long-oo /o͞o/ Spelled ou, ui

The most common spelling for the long-oo sound is oo. (See pages 67–68 for word, phrase, and sentence lists.) Less common spellings of the /o͞o/ sound include ou (soup) and ui (fruit).

/o͞o/ Spelled ou, ui Words

ou			
group	wound	cougar	**caribou**
route	you	coupon	**croutons**
soup	youth	**bayou**	**youthful**

ui			
bruise	juice	juicy	**pursuit**
cruise	suit	pantsuit	**wetsuit**
fruit	grapefruit	suitcase	

/o͞o/ Spelled ou, ui Phrases

bowl of soup	a coupon for croutons	caribou route
youth group	soup spoon	loud cougar
deep wound	river cruise	rubber wetsuit
purple bruise	hot pursuit	rolling suitcase
ruby red grapefruit	fruit juice	fancy pantsuit

/o͞o/ Spelled ou, ui Sentences

Louis took the youth group on a tour.	I lost my soup spoon in the bayou.
We drank fruit juice at the picnic.	We used a coupon to buy croutons.
My purple bruise is fading.	Would you like a bowl of soup?
The ruby red grapefruit was so juicy.	Did you hear the loud cougar cry?
We were in hot pursuit of the rolling suitcase.	We followed the caribou route into the woods.
Fay wore a fancy pantsuit on the river cruise.	Lou had stitches to close his deep wound.

-ild, -ind, -old, -olt, -ost

Words with these phonograms are sometimes referred to as "kind old words." They look like closed syllables—syllables that end in a consonant and often have a short-vowel sound—but, in fact, the vowel sound is long because of how they were originally articulated. They are of Anglo-Saxon origin. The word *kind* is one of the earliest words in the English language. You can teach these "kind old words" as word rhyming groups. Teach children this mnemonic to help them remember these word families: *M<u>ost</u> k<u>ind</u> <u>old</u> c<u>olt</u>s are m<u>ild</u>.*

-ild, -ind, -old, -olt, -ost Words

-ild			
child	mild	wild	
-ind			
bind	grind	rind	behind
blind	kind	wind	**hind**
find	mind		
-old			
bold	gold	old	sold
cold	hold	scold	told
fold	mold		
-olt			
bolt	jolt	volt	**dolt**
colt	molt		
-ost			
host	ghost	most	post

The Ultimate Book of Phonics Word Lists for Grades 1–2 © by Laurie J. Cousseau and Rhonda Graff, Scholastic Inc.

-ild, -ind, -old, -olt, -ost Phrases

hold the cold cup	mold on the rind	mild child
most kind	wild colt	bold child
lemon rind	find the colt	kind child
hold hands	a wild pony	sold for a penny
a jolt from a volt	bolt of lightning	gold ring
behind the post	will wind the kite string	fold the gold cloth
bold colt	cold gold watch	ghost at the post

-ild, -ind, -old, -olt, -ost Sentences

Do you know how to wind a clock?	They went to find the wild colt.
Let's find the pot of gold.	Hold on to the post.
The bold colt nuzzled my nose.	The gold watch was cold.
Val got a jolt from the volt.	The mild child spoke softly.
Grind the gold rocks into dust.	We went to find gold in the old mine.
This lemon rind has mold on it.	The wild colt bolted past the post.
The colt was sold to a kind lady.	A bolt of lightning split the post.
Grab the kite string before it flies away.	The ghost stood next to the old post.
The child was cold on the snowy day.	Be careful when you fold the gold cloth.
Don't forget to wind the kite string.	Kids, hold hands so no one gets left behind.

The Ultimate Book of Phonics Word Lists for Grades 1–2 © by Laurie J. Cousseau and Rhonda Graff, Scholastic Inc.

r-Controlled Vowel *ar* /är/

When *r* comes after a vowel, it changes the pronunciation of the vowel, as in *ar*.
The most common pronunciation for the spelling *ar* is /är/, as in *star*.

ar Words

arch	harm	starch	**sparkly**
arm	harp	start	**starfish**
art	jar	tart	**apartment**
bar	lard	yard	**ark**
bark	large	yarn	**argument**
barn	march	apart	**barb**
car	mark	argue	**carp**
card	marsh	artist	**chard**
cart	mart	barber	**garb**
charge	park	carpet	**harvest**
charm	part	carton	**lark**
chart	scar	charming	**par**
dark	scarf	farmer	**parch**
dart	shark	garden	**rhubarb**
far	sharp	garlic	**tar**
farm	smart	harmless	**tarp**
guard	spark	market	
hard	star	party	

ar Phrases

a bright star	a new start	at the park
a red scarf	a large bin	a dark room
a star in the dark sky	hard bark	large jar
the wet marsh	sharp dart	mark on the card
smart farmer	artist's scarf	charm in a jar
harmless shark	hidden charm	charming barber
art in the park	in the large barn	dark blue yarn

ar Sentences

Can you open the large jar?	The marsh is next to the farm.
The artist plays a magical harp.	The artist wore a sparkly scarf.
Bake a tart with rhubarb in it.	The party will start soon.
We gazed at a star far, far away.	The car in the yard will not start.
What is this mark on the card?	I found a hidden charm in the jar.
Use a tarp to protect the carton.	Carl fell off the cart and got a scar.
It's nice when they have art in the park.	The notes of the harp float up to the stars.
My scarf is made with dark blue yarn.	We grow garlic and rhubarb in the garden.
Invite the starfish and carp to the party.	The farmer has Swiss chard in his yard.
That is a very pretty charm on your arm.	The song of the lark in the marsh is lovely.

The Ultimate Book of Phonics Word Lists for Grades 1–2 © by Laurie J. Cousseau and Rhonda Graff, Scholastic Inc.

r-Controlled Vowel *or* /ôr/

When *r* comes after a vowel, it often changes the pronunciation of the vowel, as in *or*.
The most common pronunciation for the spelling *or* is /ôr/, as in *corn*.

or Words

bore	nor	sword	organize
born	north	thorn	popcorn
chore	or	tore	**core**
cord	porch	torn	**dorm**
cork	pork	wore	**glory**
corn	port	worn	**forge**
door	score	worth	**horde**
for	shore	favorite	**orbit**
force	short	florist	**organic**
fork	snore	forest	**pore**
form	sore	forty	**scorch**
fort	sort	memorize	**scorn**
forth	sport	morning	**snort**
horn	store	northeast	**swore**
horse	stork	northwest	**sworn**
more	storm	order	**torch**

r-Controlled Vowels

or Phrases

can hear the horn	a port in the northwest	flowers from the florist
fork and spoon	favorite sport	heading north
a good sport	corn on the cob	a big storm
in the fort	on the front porch	torn paper
storm in the north	organic popcorn	worth it
short fork	the Earth's orbit	loud horn
north wind	safe sport	dry corn husks

or Sentences

The storm came from the north.	Was a stork born this morning?
Rory plays a sport every fall.	His pants were worn and torn.
The storm will pass soon.	The pants are badly torn.
Be careful of the thorn.	Do you use a fork to eat popcorn?
The bike had a loud horn.	Nate sat on the porch facing north.
It is hard to eat with a short fork.	Cory went to the store to get corn.
Sort the cards so we can play.	Taking care of a horse is a chore.
George sits on the porch in the morning.	The stork landed on the fort in the forest.
We made a fort out of corn cobs and husks.	It takes the Earth one year to orbit the sun.
Can I have an order of corn on the side?	The organic popcorn was very fresh!
We found a safe port in the storm.	They made an ice fort with a large door.

The Ultimate Book of Phonics Word Lists for Grades 1–2 © by Laurie J. Cousseau and Rhonda Graff, Scholastic Inc.

r-Controlled Vowels er, ir, ur /ûr/

When r comes after a vowel, it often changes the pronunciation of the vowel, as in er, ir, and ur. The most common pronunciation for the spellings er, ir, and ur is /ûr/. This can pose a spelling challenge for children because all three spellings sound the same. To help children differentiate the spelling options, help them create fun sentences with /ûr/ words, such as: *My sister likes to turn and twirl her purple skirt.*

/ûr/ Spelled *er* Words

clerk	after	finger	otter	**butler**
fern	better	flower	over	**exert**
germ	bother	hammer	perfect	**herb**
her	brother	holler	person	**hermit**
herd	butter	lantern	river	**merge**
hers	center	layer	sister	**nerve**
perch	certain	letter	spider	**per**
perk	concert	lobster	summer	**pert**
serve	desert	monster	tiger	**simmer**
stern	dinner	mother	under	**swerve**
term	ever	never	water	**tern**
verb	expert	number	whisper	**terse**
verse	father	other	winter	**verge**

/ûr/ Spelled *er* Phrases

green fern in the center	an early dinner	a perfect day
lively verb	summer night	helpful clerk
her friendly monster	herd of horses	playful otters
stern person	fresh herbs	golden lantern
sister in the center	lovely flowers	rhyming verse
perfect person	center of the flower	red lobster

/ûr/ Spelled *er* Sentences

The stern person did not smile.	We use fresh herbs in the salad.
Please don't bother your brother.	She hit her finger with a hammer.
Flowers grow wild in the summer.	The helpful clerk gave her some tips.
The friendly monster gave her flowers.	Simmer the lobster in butter for dinner.
A herd of horses are at the center of the field.	The rhyming verse had many verbs.
A spider sat in the center of the flower.	The golden lantern lit up the summer night.
The playful otters swam near her.	I saw a green fern in the center of our yard.

/ûr/ Spelled *ir* Words

bird	girl	swirl	circle	**birch**
birth	shirt	third	circus	**flirt**
chirp	sir	thirst	dirty	**irk**
dirt	skirt	twirl	thirsty	**quirk**
fir	squirm	whirl	thirteen	**smirk**
firm	squirt	birthday	thirty	
first	stir	chirping		

/ûr/ Spelled *ir* Phrases

twirl around	a kind girl	a firm handshake
play in the dirt	twirl her skirt	a colorful bird
shirt and skirt	circle in the dirt	thirty shirts
chirping bird	thirteen birds	dirt on his shirt
the third bird	pretty skirt	first in line

The Ultimate Book of Phonics Word Lists for Grades 1–2 © by Laurie J. Cousseau and Rhonda Graff. Scholastic Inc.

/ûr/ Spelled *ir* Sentences

Thirteen birds began to chirp.	Draw a circle in the dirt.
The girl has a firm handshake.	Shirley's shirt got dirt on the hem.
The kind girl was the first to smile.	The third bird said, "Chirp."
Whirl and twirl to the music.	The girl wore a shirt and skirt.
The girl twirled and whirled her skirt.	The circus clown wore thirty shirts.
Wade wore his striped shirt to the circus.	The third girl in the line began to twirl.
We went to the circus for my birthday.	The bird found a worm under the fir tree.

/ûr/ Spelled *ur* Words

burn	curve	burger	return	**absurd**
burnt	fur	curly	Saturday	**blur**
burp	hurt	curtain	sturdy	**curt**
burst	nurse	disturb	surfboard	**hurl**
church	purr	flurry	surfer	**lurch**
churn	purse	furry	surprise	**lurk**
curb	slurp	further	Thursday	**spur**
curd	surf	gurgle	turnip	**surly**
curl	turn	purple	turtle	**urge**
curse				**urgent**

/ûr/ Spelled *ur* Phrases

curl a ribbon	Saturday surprise	in the small purse
hurt toe	curt voice	lost her surfboard
school nurse	Thursday night	curly fur
purple purse	burst of light	right turn
burst balloon	churn butter	slurp loudly

/ûr/ Spelled *ur* Sentences

The purple balloon burst.	Churn butter in an urn.
He hurt his toe on the hard curb.	Please don't slurp your drink.
He saw the school nurse about his hurt toe.	The surfer lost her surfboard in the surf.
Dad planned a Saturday surprise for us.	The surfer turned back when the storm started.
Her purple blister burst on Thursday.	Curl a ribbon and put it on your curls.

Mixed *er, ir, ur* Sentences

Her purple skirt is dirty.	The bird can turn on its perch.
The turtle and bird are friends.	The first monster to burp wins.
A friendly monster gave Shirley flowers for her birthday.	The turtle burst out of the ferns next to the purple door.
"Have you ever heard a tiger purr?" asked the turtle.	A number of birds pecked on a burger on the curb.
Thirteen otters swam in a circle and then rode the surf.	We had a surprise party for Burt's thirteenth birthday.

The Ultimate Book of Phonics Word Lists for Grades 1–2 © by Laurie J. Cousseau and Rhonda Graff, Scholastic Inc.

Suffixes -er, -or

The suffixes -er and -or can both mean "a person or thing that does," as in *painter* (a person who paints) and *actor* (a person who acts). The suffix -or is often used after a t, as in *collector* or *inventor*.

Suffix -er Words

baker	dryer	jogger	runner	washer
banker	eater	maker	singer	winner
batter	farmer	painter	sitter	writer
boater	firefighter	pitcher	swimmer	**archer**
camper	giver	player	teacher	**climber**
catcher	golfer	rapper	timer	**crooner**
dancer	helper	reader	traveler	**researcher**
drummer	hiker	rider	waiter	**welder**

Suffix -er Phrases

the master baker	the modern dancer	the strong swimmer
the expert welder	the mystery writer	teacher's helper
the hiker and climber	the drummer's concert	the brave firefighter
fast runner	pitcher and catcher	generous farmer

Suffix -er Sentences

The boater prefers a sailboat.	The pitcher and catcher played ball.
The master baker baked thirty desserts.	The farmer's rooster crowed at sunrise.
The singer was both a crooner and a rapper.	The horse rider likes to canter on the path.
The jogger never gave up going up the hill.	The rapper's version of the song won a prize.
They will place their order with the waiter.	The generous farmer gave away lots of corn.

Suffix -*or* Words

actor	editor	professor	**advisor**	**spectator**
calculator	educator	projector	**constructor**	**supervisor**
collector	inspector	sailor	**contractor**	**translator**
conductor	instructor	sculptor	**counselor**	**vendor**
decorator	inventor	survivor	**exhibitor**	
director	narrator	visitor	**protector**	

Suffix -*or* Phrases

organized supervisor	humorous instructor	decorator added glamor
supportive advisor	my favorite actor	a collector of vases
forgetful professor	important visitor	worried sailor
store inspector	bored director	a major donor

Suffix -*or* Sentences

The worried sailor checked her boat.	We have an important visitor today.
The contractor restored the old tower.	The club honored the inventor for his work.
My favorite actor performed at our school.	The students loved the humorous instructor.
The spectators ate popcorn on the stands.	The narrator read the survivor's story aloud.
Our important visitor waited on the porch.	The decorator added glamor to the room.

The Ultimate Book of Phonics Word Lists for Grades 1–2 © by Laurie J. Cousseau and Rhonda Graff, Scholastic Inc.

r-Controlled Vowels *are, air, ear* /âr/

When *r* comes after a vowel, it often changes the pronunciation of the vowel, as in *are*, *air*, and *ear*. The most common pronunciation for the spellings *are*, *air*, and *ear* is /âr/. This can pose a spelling challenge for children because all three spellings sound the same. To help children differentiate the spellings options, help them create fun sentences with /âr/ words, such as: *The bear took care as it sat on the chair.*

are, air, ear Words

are			
bare	rare	stare	**fare**
care	scare	ware	**flare**
dare	share	beware	**glare**
hare	spare	daycare	**pare**
mare	square	**blare**	**snare**

air			
air	stair	repair	**éclair**
chair	airplane	unfair	**flair**
fair	airport	upstairs	**lair**
hair	hairbrush	**disrepair**	**midair**
pair	haircut		

ear			
bear	pear	tear	wear

Mixed *are, air, ear* Phrases

airplane fare	share the éclair	fair hair
flare in midair	haircut on a dare	mares and hares
beware the bear	take care on the stairs	share at the daycare
pearl earrings	pair of pears	pear jam
can repair the tear	scare the bear	learn to wear

Mixed *are, air, ear* Sentences

The airplane fare was fair.	Beware the bear nearby.
We saw a flare in midair.	We need to repair the chair.
He seared the pear on the grill.	Smear pear jam on the bread.
She likes to wear the square scarf.	Henry got a new haircut on a dare.
The hairbrush is upstairs on the table.	Please take care on the steep stairs.
Claire shared her éclair with the mare.	Earl picked a pair of pears on the ground.
The earrings go well with her fair hair.	The kids share toys at the daycare.

Other Pronunciations for *ear*

The spelling *ear* has three pronunciations: /âr/, as in *bear*, /ēr/, as in *hear*, and /ûr/, as in *earth*. The word lists below are for the /ēr/ and /ûr/ pronunciations.

ear Pronounced /ēr/			
clear	near	earring	**gear**
dear	rear	fearless	**sear**
ear	spear	nearby	**shear**
fear	tear	yearlong	**smear**
hear	year		

ear Pronounced /ûr/			
earl	heard	search	**yearn**
earn	learn	earthworm	
earth	pearl	searchlight	

Long *oo* /ōo/ and **Short *oo* /ŏo/**

The vowel team *oo* has two pronunciations: long /ōo/, as in *moon*, and short /ŏo/, as in *book*. A mnemonic you might want to teach children could be: *Let's read a book on the moon.*

Long *oo* /ōo/ Words

bloom	hoop	school	tool	raccoon
boo	hoot	scoop	tooth	rooster
boot	loon	shoo	afternoon	shampoo
broom	loop	shoot	baboon	spooky
choose	loose	smooth	balloon	sunroom
coo	moo	snooze	cartoon	**bamboo**
cool	mood	soon	doodle	**boon**
coop	moon	spook	gloomy	**croon**
drool	moose	spool	goofy	**doom**
food	noon	spoon	kangaroo	**droop**
fool	pool	stool	lagoon	**gloom**
goose	roof	stoop	mushroom	**loom**
groom	room	swoop	noodles	**moonbeam**
groove	roost	too	poodle	**woo**

Long *oo* /ōo/ Phrases

loose tooth	goofy poodle	rooster coop
full moon	bamboo broom	loon in the lagoon
spooky room	cool raccoon	cool pool
loose goose	toot-toot	silver spoon
gloomy day	smooth stone	in the mood for food

Complex Vowels

Long *oo* /ōō/ Sentences

Soon it will be noon.	The raccoon ate all the food.
Shoo the goose away from the sunroom.	I cleaned the room with a bamboo broom.
My tooth came loose because I ate hard food.	The cartoon show had a cool raccoon.
The loon in the lagoon will soon swim away.	The hens cooed at the rooster in the coop.
The goofy poodle drooled in my room.	The moose will snooze in the afternoon.
Use the silver spoon to scoop up the food.	The school team will shoot hoops at noon.
The owl said "hoot" as it flew to its roost.	The goofy baboon flew in a hot-air balloon.

Short *oo* /ŏŏ/ Words

book	hoof	wood	cookie	understood
brook	hook	woof	fishhook	wooden
cook	look	wool	football	woodpile
crook	nook	barefoot	footprint	**footloose**
foot	shook	bookcase	goodbye	**rook**
good	stood	bookshelf	notebook	**rookie**
hood	took	cookbook	redwood	**soot**

Short *oo* /oͦo/ Phrases

good book	stood barefoot	torn notebook
took wood	horse's hoof	curved fishhook
scratchy wool	good cook	secret nook
sharp hook	soot on my foot	footprint in the sand

Short *oo* /oͦo/ Sentences

I took wood to the campfire to cook.	The cook stood on his feet all day.
My sweater is made of scratchy wool.	The good cook made nutmeg cookies.
I read a good book in my secret nook.	We stood in the sandy footprints.
The horse's hoof needed to be trimmed.	She stood barefoot in the redwood forest.
The soot from the wood got on my foot.	Look, the torn notebook is on the bookshelf.
The car's hood looks good after we washed it.	We used a curved fishhook at the brook.

Mixed Long and Short *oo* Sentences

We read a good book about the moon.	"Woof," said the poodle and drooled.
The cook took the mushrooms from the room.	Which footprint belongs to the large moose?
Brooke tied a loop around the fishhook.	The loon stood on the bookcase in my room.
I took a scoop of noodles from the bowl.	The book is about a moose and a goose.
We used bamboo to make a wooden stool.	The kangaroo stood tall to look around.

au, aw /ô/

The letters *au* and *aw* are the most common spellings of the broad-*o* sound /ô/. The spelling *au* can be found at the beginning of a word, as in *autumn*, or in the middle, as in *sauce*. The spelling *aw* is often found at the end of a word, as in *jaw*. It can also be followed by the letter *n*, as *lawn*, or the letter *l*, as in *shawl*. Teach children this mnemonic to help them remember the spellings *au* and *aw*: *I saw a hawk in autumn.*

au, aw Words

au			
caught	sauce	daughter	**audit**
cause	taught	dinosaur	**clause**
fault	audience	faucet	**fraud**
haul	August	laundry	**jaunt**
haunt	author	saucer	**vault**
launch	autumn	sausage	
pause	because		

aw			
awe	lawn	thaw	**awning**
claw	paw	yawn	**bawl**
crawl	raw	awesome	**brawl**
dawn	saw	awful	**drawl**
draw	scrawl	coleslaw	**flaw**
drawn	shawl	drawing	**gawky**
fawn	slaw	lawyer	**gnaw**
hawk	sprawl	sawdust	**pawn**
jaw	squawk	strawberry	
law	straw		

au, aw Phrases

the month of August	tomato sauce	cup and saucer
leaky faucet	locked vault	pork sausage
long pause	clean laundry	launch pad
dawn to dusk	buttery sauce	awful day
bear paw	wide yawn	gawky bird
a fawn and a hawk	straw on the lawn	saw the hawk
autumn leaves	dirty paws	sauce with sausage

au, aw Sentences

The crow cried "caw" at dawn.	Paul's drawing looks awesome.
The hawk let out a squawk.	The rocket launched off at dawn.
Some autumn leaves are yellow.	The dog had dirty paws.
The month of August can be awfully hot.	We ate lobster with buttery sauce.
Mom fixed the leaky faucet in the laundry.	My jaw is tired from yawning all afternoon.
We worked without pause from dawn to dusk.	The faucet broke, but it's not my fault.
Draw a picture of the cup and saucer.	The lawyer kept papers in a locked vault.
The gawky bird looks like a small dinosaur.	The audience yawned a lot during the show.

The words **awe** and **awesome** have an *e* after the *aw* because of the origin of the word. It means "filled with wonder." The *e* distinguishes it from the root "aw," as in *awful,* which has a negative connotation. Both words derive from Old English.

Diphthongs *oi*, *oy* /oi/

The /oi/ sound is a diphthong and is commonly spelled *oi* or *oy*. A diphthong, or sliding vowel combination, starts with one sound and glides into another. The spelling *oi* often appears in the beginning of a word, as in *oil*, or in the middle, as in *coin*. The spelling *oy* is more likely to appear at the end of a word, as in *joy*. A helpful mnemonic that uses both spellings is *joyful noise*.

oi, *oy* Words

oi			
boil	moist	avoid	**joist**
broil	noise	moisture	**ointment**
choice	oil	noisy	**poise**
coil	point	poison	**rejoice**
coin	soil	**exploit**	**thyroid**
foil	spoil	**foist**	**turmoil**
join	toil	**hoist**	**void**
joint	voice		

oy			
boy	cowboy	loyal	**decoy**
joy	destroy	royal	**employ**
toy	enjoy	voyage	**ploy**
annoy	joyful	**coy**	**soy**

The Ultimate Book of Phonics Word Lists for Grades 1–2 © by Laurie J. Cousseau and Rhonda Graff Scholastic Inc.

oi, oy Phrases

destroy the foil	moist air	joyful noise
pride and joy	coin toss	loyal friend
quiet voice	boiling water	join in the noise
moist soil	enjoy the voyage	noisy toy
spoil their joy	boy's toy	will annoy the boy
can point to the coin	spoiled soil	loud voices
noisy cowboys	gold coins	coiled snake

oi, oy Sentences

Put the noisy toy in the oil.	That shy boy is a loyal friend.
We will join the noisy singing.	The coiled snake lay on the wall.
The loud voices were full of joy.	The soil was spoiled with trash.
Enjoy the salad with olive oil.	Moist soil is good for most plants.
My collection of coins is my pride and joy.	She spoke in a quiet voice to avoid noise.
We found the coins deep in the soil.	Coil the rope and join the ends together.
Don't destroy the foil after you use it.	Please point to the toy you would like.
The boy wanted to enjoy the voyage.	Our team rejoiced when we won the coin toss.

Diphthongs *ou*, *ow* /ou/

The /ou/ sound is a diphthong and is commonly spelled *ou* or *ow*. A diphthong, or sliding vowel combination, starts with one sound and glides into another. The spelling *ou* often appears at the beginning of a word, as in *out*, or in the middle, as in *loud*. The spelling *ow* is more likely to appear at the end of a word, as in *cow*. A helpful mnemonic that uses both spellings is *loud cow*.

> The spelling *ou* can stand for different sounds, including: /ou/, as in *ouch*; long /oo/, as in *soup*; short /ŭ/, as in *cousin*; and long /ō/, as in *shoulder*.

/ou/ Spelled *ou* Words

blouse	hound	pouch	sprout	**crouch**
bounce	house	pound	trout	**douse**
cloud	loud	pout	about	**flounce**
couch	mound	proud	flounder	**grouse**
count	mount	round	grouchy	**pounce**
doubt	mouse	scout	mountain	**scour**
flour	mouth	shout	outgrow	**shroud**
foul	noun	sound	outside	**snout**
found	ouch	sour	thousand	**stout**
grouch	ounce	south	**bound**	
ground	out	spout	**bout**	

/ou/ Spelled *ou* Phrases

stout mouse	clouds in the south	bounce and shout
grouchy hound	round snout	proud grouse
found a pouch	loud sound	mouse in the house
crouch to the ground	shrouded by clouds	lost pouch
trout and flounder	hike up the mountain	count the nouns

/ou/ Spelled *ou* Sentences

The grouchy hound has a round snout.	The scouts hiked up the mountain.
Don't pout; dance and shout!	Piper found a pouch of sour candy.
We lay on the ground to count clouds.	The mouse crouched to the ground.
The cats found a mouse in the house.	Don't bounce on the couch!
The family will outgrow that house.	Fran scoured the pantry for flour.
With a pounce, the proud mouse went south.	The mountain peak was shrouded by clouds.
	We found the lost pouch on the ground.
	Dad cooked trout and flounder for dinner.

> The spelling *ow* can stand for different sounds, including: /ou/, as in *now*, and long /ō/, as in *grow*.

/ou/ Spelled *ow* Words

bow	drown	owl	powder	**browse**
brown	fowl	plow	power	**dowel**
chow	frown	town	rowdy	**jowl**
clown	gown	wow	shower	**pow**
cow	growl	yowl	snowplow	**prowl**
crowd	how	allow	towel	**scowl**
crown	howl	chowder	tower	**sow**
down	now	downtown	**brow**	**vow**

/ou/ Spelled *ow* Phrases

corn chowder	crowded town	Farmer Brown
the brown owl	yowl and growl	rowdy crowd
power downtown	crown and gown	tall towers
plow the field now	bow to the crowd	cats on the prowl
cats on the prowl	wet towel	growl at the snowplow

/ou/ Spelled *ow* Sentences

The wet towel hangs on a dowel.	The clown bowed to the crowd.
Her satin gown was powder blue.	The brown owl heard a howl.
Her crown matched her golden gown.	My dog growled at the big snowplow.
Wow, this corn chowder tastes great!	The brown owl hooted in the trees.
"Ow," I yelled as I hit my brow in the shower.	The cats yowl and growl while on the prowl.
The cows scowled at the fowl on the field.	Farmer Brown plans to plow the field now.
We can browse at the bookstore downtown.	How did the brown cow wow the crowd?

Mixed *ou, ow* Phrases

brown snout	drowsy hound	grouchy clown
flower sprouted	the stout owl	proud sow
crowded couch	scouring powder	down south
frown at the mouse	bounty of wildflowers	loud meow
power out	owl crouched	

Mixed *ou, ow* Sentences

The cow has a round, brown snout.	The power went out downtown.
A bounty of wildflowers sprouted.	The countess frowned at the mouse.
A flower sprouted from the dry ground.	The stout owl crouched on the ground.
The drowsy hound curled up on the couch.	Clean the counter with scouring powder.
The grouchy clown wore a brown blouse.	A loud meow woke up the fowl on the mound.

Schwa

Schwa /ə/ is the most common vowel sound in the English language. In a multisyllabic word, we often hear the schwa sound in an unstressed syllable. The schwa sound can be spelled with any vowel. The vowel does not stand for either its long or short sound. Instead, the vowel sound may be closer to short /ŭ/ or /ĭ/. That makes spelling words with a schwa sound challenging for children.

Start by introducing the schwa sound that is spelled with the letter *a*, as in *about* or *again*. The word *banana* has three *a*s. The first and third syllables have the schwa sound. Once children are familiar with schwa, introduce additional examples over time. For example, the suffixes *-al* and *-en* are also pronounced with a schwa vowel sound, as in the words *pedal* or *golden*.

> In a multisyllabic word with three syllables, the medial syllable is often unstressed. The schwa sound falls in this syllable.

Schwa *a* Words

Schwa *a* (at the beginning of a word)				
about	agree	amaze	applause	awake
above	ahead	aamong	ashamed	aware
adapt	alarm	amount	ashore	away
adult	Alaska	annoy	aside	awoke
afraid	alive	another	asleep	
again	alone	apart	avoid	
ago	along	appear	await	

Schwa *a* (in the middle or at the end of a word)				
banana	extra	pasta	scuba	zebra
camera	human	pedal	tuba	parka
central	oval	postal	tuna	tundra
comma	panda	royal	yoga	vista

Schwa *a* Phrases

Eva the zebra	Marla the panda	go away
extra bananas	appear annoyed	afraid of the panda
another alarm	pasta with tuna	camera broke again
amazing humans	postal stamp	applause for the tuba
amount of bananas	warm parka	Alaskan tundra

Schwa *a* Sentences

I'm annoyed the camera broke again.	We have a large amount of bananas.
Velma likes pasta with tuna.	Do you have another alarm?
Eva the zebra and Marla the panda do yoga.	There's a new postal stamp with a panda.
Wear a warm parka at the Alaskan tundra.	There was a big applause for the tuba solo.
Anna wore an oval opal around her neck.	"Go away," said the zebra who was asleep.

Schwa *e* Words

aspen	eaten	helmet	model	sunken
basket	eleven	item	pocket	taken
blanket	even	jacket	present	telephone
broken	fallen	kitten	problem	travel
camel	freshen	linen	raven	trumpet
carpet	frozen	listen	rotten	woolen
chicken	garden	locket	seven	**freshmen**
children	golden	magnet	sherbet	**garnet**
dampen	happen	mitten	silent	**token**
darken	harden			

Schwa *e* Phrases

eleven kittens	golden chicken	woolen mitten
golden token	freshened blanket	fallen aspen
sunken ship	sunken garden	seven children
raven's feather	broken magnet	frozen rain
listen to the trumpet	rotten problem	item in the pocket

Schwa *e* Sentences

The golden chicken won the prize.	Do not walk on the frozen lake.
If you dampen the linen, it will darken.	The raven sat on the broken fence.
We like to listen to music in the garden.	What happened to the golden token?
Moths have eaten my woolen mittens!	Garnets were found in the sunken ship.
Eleven kittens are sleeping in the garden.	The frozen rain hardened the garden soil.
The fallen aspen tree had a rotten trunk.	Hang the blanket outdoors to freshen it.

Schwa (Mixed Vowels) Words

Schwa *i*				
animal	direct	pencil	**cavity**	**imitate**
April	divide	president	**decimal**	**indicate**
basin	family	pupil	**fossil**	**medical**
cousin	holiday	raisin	**hesitate**	
Schwa *o*				
blossom	confide	lemon	parrot	reason
bottom	cotton	lesson	person	**atom**
comfort	content	melon	pilot	**carbon**
common	falcon	other	season	**crimson**

The Ultimate Book of Phonics Word Lists for Grades 1–2 © by Laurie J. Cousseau and Rhonda Graff. Scholastic Inc.

Schwa (Mixed Vowels) Phrases

bottom of the basket	eaten pasta	frozen tundra
busy family	oval locket	lemon sherbet
cotton jacket	crimson pencil	extra pocket
supply of melons	children murmur	holiday season
pencils for pupils	focus on problem	walrus has cavity
eleven minus seven	April blossoms	animals in Alaska
animal crackers	ripe banana	frozen blossoms
extra jackets	seven animals	silent parrots

Schwa (Mixed Vowels) Sentences

Have you seen my crimson pencil?	The parrot sat upon the cactus.
We had animal crackers for a snack.	The ripe bananas were mushy.
Lucy wears her oval locket every day.	The walrus has a cavity in its tooth.
The kittens hid in the bottom of the basket.	Lemon sherbet is my favorite dessert.
We have eaten pasta for seven days in a row!	Name some animals that live in Alaska.
When you sharpen a pencil, you shorten it.	Cole has a cotton jacket with an extra pocket.
We need a bunch of pencils for the pupils.	Focus on the math problem on the board.
In the winter, the blossoms were frozen.	We needed extra jackets because it was cold.

The Ultimate Book of Phonics Word Lists for Grades 1–2 © by Laurie J. Cousseau and Rhonda Graff, Scholastic Inc.

Silent-Letter Teams

Silent-letter teams consist of two consonants of which one is pronounced and the other is silent, such as *kn* /n/, as in *knee*; *wr* /r/, as in *wrist*; *rh* /r/, as in *rhyme*; and *mb* /m/, as in *thumb*. In Old English, both consonants were originally pronounced, but over time one sound was omitted for ease of pronunciation. For example, *knight* would have been /k/ /n/ /ī/ /t/.

kn Words

knee	knit	knapsack	**knave**
kneel	knob	kneecap	**knead**
knelt	knock	knowledge	**knickknacks**
knife	knot	knuckles	**knoll**
knight	know		

kn Phrases

knitting in knots	a knight on his knees	a nifty knife
a grassy knoll	dirty kneecaps	a knit knapsack
lots of knickknacks	knead dough	shiny doorknob
knock-knock	scraped knuckles	knelt on the grass

kn Sentences

Ken likes to tell "knock-knock" jokes.	The knitting was tangled in knots.
The knight has a knack for knitting.	The clever knave knows how to knit.
Please knock on the door and turn the knob.	The knights knelt in the knoll.
The heavy knapsack knocked down the fence.	Mom kneads the dough with her knuckles.
The knight hurt his kneecaps while riding.	Ned's knees began to knock together.

wr Words

wrap	wrist	wrestle	writer	**wring**
wreath	write	wrestling	writing	**wrought**
wreck	wrong	wriggle	written	
wren	wrote	wrinkle	**wrangle**	
wrench	wrapping	wristwatch	**wrath**	

wr Phrases

a broken wrist	wrinkled wrapping paper	wrap up your writing
the gold wristwatch	singing wren	evergreen wreath
wrong paper	wrestling match	wrangle horses

wr Sentences

It's time to wrap up your writing.	Wright wore the gold wristwatch.
I cannot write with a broken wrist.	The wrought iron fence is wrecked.
The cowgirl wrangled the horses.	The floor was a wreck after wrestling.
The singing wren perched on the wreath.	It is hard to wrangle the wriggling fish.

Many words that start with *wr* are often associated with a twisting motion, as in *write*, *wrestle*, and *wriggle*.

rh Words

rhyme	rhinoceros	rhythmic	**rhinestone**	**rhombus**
rhino	rhythm	**rhapsody**	**rhododendron**	**rhubarb**

rh Phrases

rhythmic rhino	rhythm of the rhymes	colorful rhododendron
rhombus shape	rhinoceros's horn	lovely rhapsody
fresh rhubarb	bright rhinestone	rhyme time

The Ultimate Book of Phonics Word Lists for Grades 1–2 © by Laurie J. Cousseau and Rhonda Graff Scholastic Inc.

rh Sentences

Rhea recites rhythmic rhymes.	The rhino ate rhubarb with Rhonda.
The lovely rhapsody lulled me to sleep.	Rhoda wore a bright rhinestone.
We picked rhododendrons in Rhode Island.	A square is a rhombus with four equal sides.
Kids love rhyme time during reading class.	Listen to the rhythm of the rhymes.

-mb Words

climb	lamb	thumb	**doorjamb**
comb	limb	plumber	**tomb**
crumb	numb	thumbnail	

-mb Phrases

out on a limb	skilled plumber	wooly lamb
limbs of the tree	numb thumb	crusty crumbs
mummy's tomb	broken comb	plumber fix
can climb a tree	hair comb	crumbs on the table

-mb Sentences

A fish can't climb a tree.	The comb got stuck in my hair.
There were crumbs on the table.	The lamb is soft and furry.
She likes to comb the lamb's wool.	The mummy's tomb is in the museum.
His thumb got caught in the doorjamb.	We climbed up the limbs of the tree.
I hurt my thumb on the broken comb.	The plumber fixed the leaky sink.
Her limb was numb from sitting on the floor.	There were crusty crumbs left on the plate.

Contractions

A *contraction* is a shorter form of two words that are joined together. An apostrophe takes the place of the missing letter(s), which is usually a vowel. For example, in the contraction *isn't* (is + not), the apostrophe replaces the *o*. In the contraction *I'm* (I + am), the apostrophe replaces the *a*.

Many people confuse *it's* and *its*. *It's* is a contraction of "it is." Have children replace *it's* with *it is* to see if the sentence still makes sense. (For example: *It's a sunny day. It is a sunny day.*)

The word *its* is a possessive pronoun that means "belong to." (For example: *The dog chased its tail.*)

Contraction Words

are				
they're	we're	who're	you're	
have				
I've	they've	we've	what've	you've
is				
he's	it's	that's	what's	who's
how's	she's	there's	where's	
not				
aren't	didn't	hadn't	isn't	weren't
can't	doesn't	hasn't	shouldn't	won't*
couldn't	don't	haven't	wasn't	wouldn't
will				
he'll	it'll	they'll	who'll	
I'll	she'll	we'll	you'll	
would or *had*				
I'd	she'd	we'd	you'd	
he'd	they'd	who'd		
us				
let's				

* The word *won't* is a contraction of "will not." In the 16th century the word for "will not" was *wonnot*, which became *won't* in modern 17th-century English. Doesn't that make it clearer where the *o* comes from?

Adding Suffixes
(with no change to the base word)

Suffixes are word parts that come at the end of a word and can change the word's tense, meaning, and/or part of speech. For example, *plant/planted* denotes a change from present tense to past tense. *Hope/hopeless* denotes a change in meaning. Although the word *wind* is a noun, when we add *-y* at the end, it becomes an adjective, *windy*. (Note: You might want to introduce children to the four main parts of speech: noun [namer], adjective [describer], verb [action], and adverb [how]. Keep this introduction to grammar simple and functional, connecting them to sentence structure.)

When introducing suffixes to young learners, choose ones that have concrete meanings and do not require any change of spelling to the base word, such as *jumping*, *planted*, or *singer*. As children gain experience using suffixes, they will see that different suffixes can be added to the same base word; for example, *prevent*, *prevented*, *preventing*, and *prevention*. In addition, some words can have more than one suffix, such as *hopefully*.

Suffixes	Meaning/Usage	Part of Speech	Word Examples
-ed	past tense	verb; adjective	*planted, pulled, fished*
-en	quality of	adjective	*wooden*
-er	person who; comparing two things	noun; adjective	*farmer* *longer*
-est	comparing three or more	adjective	*longest*
-ing	happening in the moment	verb; adjective; noun	I am *talking*. I was *talking*. I will be *talking*.
-ly	answers the question "how?"	adverb	spoke *slowly*
-s/-es	plural; present tense	noun; verb	*cats* *wishes*
-y	describing	adjective	*windy*

Suffix Spelling Rule #1: Drop e

After children have worked with various suffixes and practiced adding them to base words that do not require any spelling change (e.g., *farm + er*), they are ready for words that do require a change to the base word when suffixes are added. Introduce these three spelling rules for adding suffixes: Drop *e*, Double the Final Consonant, and Change *y* to *i*.

The Drop *e* spelling rule is easiest to remember with these two checkpoints:

Checkpoint 1: The base word ends with an *e*. Drop the *e* on the base word when adding a suffix that begins with a vowel (including *e*).

Checkpoint 2: The suffix begins with a vowel. If the suffix begins with a consonant, keep the *e* on the base word.

Help children understand that even after the suffix is added, the *e* is still technically part of the base word and is still doing its job of making the vowel long. Tell children the *e* is "hiding" behind the suffix. For example, when we add *-ing* to *slide*, we may say we "drop the *e*" but the *e* is actually "hiding" behind the *-ing*, so the *i* sound in *sliding* is still long. Some children may find this confusing, so it is helpful to spend some time practicing it. (Note: Not all words that end with *e* have a long-vowel sound.)

Drop *e* Words (Suffix begins with a vowel)

-ed			
bake + ed = baked	file + ed = filed	note + ed = noted	swipe + ed = swiped
change + ed = changed	hike + ed = hiked	place + ed = placed	theme + ed = themed
chase + ed = chased	invite + ed = invited	save + ed = saved	trade + ed = traded
close + ed = closed	like + ed = liked	scrape + ed = scraped	use + ed = used
dine + ed = dined	love + ed = loved	share + ed = shared	vote + ed = voted
dislike + ed = disliked	mute + ed = muted	smile + ed = smiled	wave + ed = waved
excuse + ed = excused	name + ed = named	stripe + ed = striped	wipe + ed = wiped
-er			
bake + er = baker	dive + er = diver	ride + er = rider	time + er = timer
bike + er = biker	drive + er = driver	skate + er = skater	trade + er = trader
dance + er = dancer	joke + er = joker	slice + er = slicer	write + er = writer

-est			
brave + est = bravest	cute + est = cutest	late + est = latest	tame + est = tamest
close + est = closest	huge + est = hugest	safe + est = safest	wide + est = widest

-ing			
amaze + ing = amazing	confuse + ing = confusing	invite + ing = inviting	shake + ing = shaking
bake + ing = baking	dance + ing = dancing	live + ing = living	shine + ing = shining
bite + ing = biting	date + ing = dating	love + ing = loving	slope + ing = sloping
blame + ing = blaming	describe + ing = describing	make + ing = making	strike + ing = striking
blaze + ing = blazing	dine + ing = dining	paste + ing = pasting	take + ing = taking
come + ing = coming	escape + ing = escaping	quote + ing = quoting	twinkle + ing = twinkling
compete + ing = competing	glide + ing = gliding	rake + ing = raking	use + ing = using
compose + ing = composing	hide + ing = hiding	rise + ing = rising	wave + ing = waving

-y			
bone + y = bony	grime + y = grimy	noise + y = noisy	smoke + y = smoky
bounce + y = bouncy	haze + y = hazy	scare + y = scary	spice + y = spicy
breeze + y = breezy	ice + y = icy	shade + y = shady	spine + y = spiny
craze + y = crazy	juice + y = juicy	shine + y = shiny	taste + y = tasty
ease + y = easy	lace + y = lacy	slime + y = slimy	wave + y = wavy

Suffixes

Drop *e* Phrases

waved hello	voted today	smiled at her friend
chased the cat	saved me a seat	traded baseball cards
scraped a knee	baked a cake	shared desserts
a fast skater	good writer	slowest driver
cutest puppy	latest book	widest river
making dessert	shining sun	dining out tonight
baking a pie	hiding behind	taking a break
dancing wildly	twinkling stars	the rising sun
sloping hill	raking leaves	biting an apple
noisy party	shady spot	slimy worms
breezy day	lacy fabric	a shiny ring

Drop *e* Sentences

The driver went slowly.	My uncle baked a cake.
The noisy party lasted until dawn.	I shared some news with my friends.
Nicole is a very good novel writer.	We wiped the seats clean.
We shared the yummy dessert.	Lily saved me a seat for the concert.
They chose the cutest puppy.	Mitch and Sage hiked last week.
We were dancing wildly at sunset.	We found a nice shady spot under an elm tree.
The hedgehog was hiding in the woods.	We used slimy worms to catch many fish.
The pink dress is made of lacy fabric.	We loved watching the twinkling stars.
Alex baked an apple pie for the picnic.	Carla voted today and got a colorful sticker.

The Ultimate Book of Phonics Word Lists for Grades 1–2 © by Laurie J. Cousseau and Rhonda Graff, Scholastic Inc.

Keep the *e* Words (Suffix begins with a consonant)

-ful			
care + ful = careful	hope + ful = hopeful	plate + ful = plateful	use + ful = useful
grace + ful = graceful	peace + ful = peaceful	taste + ful = tasteful	wake + ful = wakeful

-less			
care + less = careless	name + less = nameless	shame + less = shameless	tire + less = tireless
hope + less = hopeless	price + less = priceless	time + less = timeless	use + less = useless

-ly			
close + ly = closely	like + ly = likely	name + ly = namely	sure + ly = surely
extreme + ly = extremely	lone + ly = lonely	nice + ly = nicely	time + ly = timely
late + ly = lately	love + ly = lovely	strange + ly = strangely	wise + ly = wisely

-ment			
agree + ment = agreement	excite + ment = excitement	measure + ment = measurement	replace + ment = replacement
amaze + ment = amazement	manage + ment = management	move + ment = movement	state + ment = statement

-ness			
close + ness = closeness	late + ness = lateness	ripe + ness = ripeness	stale + ness = staleness
cute + ness = cuteness	like + ness = likeness	rude + ness = rudeness	wide + ness = wideness

-s			
age + s = ages	kite + s = kites	plane + s = planes	write + s = writes
bake + s = bakes	mane + s = manes	store + s = stores	zone + s = zones

Keep the *e* Phrases

graceful dancer	a useful tool	a plateful of rice
feeling hopeless	a priceless moment	careless worker
closely watched	wild excitement	strangely quiet
wisely made a choice	exact measurements	extreme amazement
amazing likeness	closeness of the sisters	lateness of the guest
open stores	writes a story	flies kites

Keep the *e* Sentences

Do not be a careless worker.	It was extremely hot.
It is useful to have bags in the car.	The class was strangely quiet.
Jake was not lonely when his friends came.	He was extremely grateful for their gift.
The graceful dancer spun and twirled.	Hopeful thinking may lead to positive results.
There was wild excitement before the concert.	A plateful of rice and beans sounds yummy.
We need exact measurements in cooking.	We closely watched the hatching eggs.

Suffix Spelling Rule #2:
Double the Final Consonant

The Double the Final Consonant spelling rule is easiest to remember when approached with four checkpoints:

Checkpoint 1: The base word ends with a single consonant.

Checkpoint 2: The base word has a single short vowel.

Checkpoint 3: The base word is one syllable.

Checkpoint 4: The suffix begins with a vowel.

When all four checkpoints are met, double the final consonant on the base word when adding the vowel suffix. This protects the short vowel in the first syllable, keeping its sound short. If not protected, the first syllable might be open, with a long-vowel sound.

Provide opportunities for children to build words by adding suffixes to base words and deconstruct words by isolating base words and suffixes.

Double the Final Consonant Words

-ed			
bat + ed = batted	drop + ed = dropped	mop + ed = mopped	stop + ed = stopped
chat + ed = chatted	flip + ed = flipped	scrub + ed = scrubbed	tap + ed = tapped
clap + ed = clapped	grab + ed = grabbed	shop + ed = shopped	trip + ed = tripped
dot + ed = dotted	grip + ed = gripped	skid + ed = skidded	tug + ed = tugged
drag + ed = dragged	hop + ed = hopped	skip + ed = skipped	wag + ed = wagged
drip + ed = dripped	map + ed = mapped	snap + ed = snapped	zip + ed = zipped
-er			
bat + er = batter	flat + er = flatter	spin + er = spinner	win + er = winner
drum + er = drummer	jog + er = jogger	swim + er = swimmer	wrap + er = wrapper
fat + er = fatter	run + er = runner	thin + er = thinner	zip + er = zipper
-est			
big + est = biggest	fit + est = fittest	hot + est = hottest	sad + est = saddest
dim + est = dimmest	flat + est = flattest	mad + est = maddest	thin + est = thinnest

-ing			
chop + ing = chopping	hug + ing = hugging	rip + ing = ripping	slip + ing = slipping
dig + ing = digging	jam + ing = jamming	run + ing = running	spin + ing = spinning
dip + ing = dipping	pet + ing = petting	ship + ing = shipping	step + ing = stepping
drip + ing = dripping	plan + ing = planning	shop + ing = shopping	tug + ing = tugging
grin + ing = grinning	quit + ing = quitting	sit + ing = sitting	win + ing = winning

-y			
drip + y = drippy	fun + y = funny	nut + y = nutty	snip + y = snippy
flop + y = floppy	grit + y = gritty	run + y = runny	star + y = starry
fog + y = foggy	mud + y = muddy	shag + y = shaggy	wit + y = witty

Do NOT Double the Consonant (if any of the checkpoints is not met)

The base word ends with two consonants.			
colder	missed	restless	trusting
fishing	painted	sorted	wanted
jumping	planted	starting	wished
lifted	pressed	taller	yelled
The base word has two vowels.			
coolest	looked	reading	trained
floated	moaned	speaking	waiting
The suffix begins with a consonant.			
badly	gladness	runs	spotless
cupful	lovely	shipment	stars
dimly	maps		
Extra: The letter x is never doubled.			
boxer	fixing	taxed	waxes

Double the Final Consonant Phrases

biggest rabbit	grabbed a snack	muddy feet
dripped water	grinning widely	planning a trip
foggy morning	hopped along	funny story
gritty taste	swift runner	strong swimmer
snapped twig	spinning quickly	starry night sky
a muddy puddle	wagged his tail	skipped down the road
flatter than paper	zipped a zipper	shopped for clothes
a swimmer's victory	dropped the plate	petting the pup
slipping on ice	a talented drummer	mopped up the mess

Double the Final Consonant Sentences

The jogger ran with his shaggy dog.	We gazed up at the starry night sky.
It was a misty and foggy morning.	I had a gritty taste in my mouth.
Dom dripped water on the floor.	The kids jumped in the muddy puddle.
We chatted as we were chopping wood.	He hopped and skipped along the path.
Rose saw the biggest rabbit in the grass.	We were grinning after winning the race.
Sandra is a swift runner and strong swimmer.	We planned the trip and mapped our way.
We grabbed a snack and headed home.	I tripped over a snapped twig on the path.
Mark dragged his sleeve over his runny nose.	After school, Theo shopped for cleats.

Suffix Spelling Rule #3: Change *y* to *i*

This Change *y* to *i* spelling rule is easiest to remember when approached with two checkpoints.

Checkpoint 1: The base word ends with a *y*.

Checkpoint 2: The letter before the *y* is a consonant.

Change the *y* to an *i* when adding a suffix, whether it begins with a vowel or consonant.

Do not change *y* to *i* when:

- the suffix begins with an *i*, such as *-ing* or *-ish*.
- there is a vowel before the *y*, such as *ay*, *ey*, or *oy*.

Provide opportunities for children to build words by adding suffixes to base words and deconstruct words by isolating base words and suffixes.

Change *y* to *i* Words

-ed			
carry + ed = carried	dry + ed = dried	marry + ed = married	study + ed = studied
cry + ed = cried	hurry + ed = hurried	reply + ed = replied	try + ed = tried
-er			
busy + er = busier	happy + er = happier	funny + er = funnier	lucky + er = luckier
carry + er = carrier	fly + er = flier	icy + er = icier	pretty + er = prettier
-es			
baby + es = babies	country + es = countries	lady + es = ladies	pony + es = ponies
bunny + es = bunnies	factory + es = factories	lily + es = lilies	puppy + es = puppies
city + es = cities	family + es = families	party + es = parties	sky + es = skies
copy + es = copies	fry + es = fries	penny + es = pennies	spy + es = spies
-est			
bumpy + est = bumpiest	cozy + est = coziest	funny + est = funniest	silly + est = silliest
busy + est = busiest	cuddly + est = cuddliest	lucky + est = luckiest	tiny + est = tiniest

The Ultimate Book of Phonics Word Lists for Grades 1–2 © by Laurie J. Cousseau and Rhonda Graff, Scholastic Inc.

	-ful		
beauty + ful = beautiful	duty + ful = dutiful	mercy + ful = merciful	plenty + ful = plentiful
bounty + ful = bountiful	fancy + ful = fanciful	pity + ful = pitiful	

	-ness		
bossy + ness = bossiness	happy + ness = happiness	lazy + ness = laziness	silly + ness = silliness
cozy + ness = coziness	icy + ness = iciness	lonely + ness = loneliness	windy + ness = windiness

	-ous		
envy + ous = envious	glory + ous = glorious	harmony + ous = harmonious	study + ous = studious

Do NOT Change the *y* to *i* (if any of the checkpoints is not met)

Do not change the *y* if the suffix begins with an *i*.			
babyish	crying	grayish	spying
boyish	drying	hurrying	studying
copying	emptying	puppyish	trying
Do not change the *y* if there is a vowel before the *y*.			
boys	enjoyment	obeyed	sprayer
chimneys	journeys	player	toys
delayed	joyful	playful	trays
displayed	keys	pulleys	turkeys
donkeys	monkeys	relayed	valleys

Suffixes

Change *y* to *i* Phrases

beautiful babies	funniest joke	tiniest ponies
studied hard	coziest chair	bumpiest ride
secret spies	cuddliest bunnies	french fries
many countries	starry skies	carried the puppies
makes some copies	visiting the ladies	the coziest blanket
extreme happiness	invited to the parties	collecting pennies
tried to be careful	watching the bunnies	a plentiful harvest
funnier than ever	the luckiest kid	working at the factories

Change *y* to *i* Sentences

We have the cuddliest bunnies.	We sat under the starry skies.
There were so many beautiful babies to hold.	We saw the tiniest ponies at the farm.
Ben studied very hard to set up a business.	We had the bumpiest ride without a saddle.
The secret spies hid in the tiniest space.	Hot french fries taste so good with salt.
He told the funniest joke and we all giggled.	The ladies plan to visit many countries.
Carlos found the coziest chair to read in.	They carried the sweet puppies in a basket.

96

Homophones

Homophones are words that sound the same but have different meanings or spellings.

Homophone Words

ate / eight	fair / fare	new / knew	sell / cell
be / bee	for / four	not / knot	so / sew
bear / bare	gate / gait	our / hour	steel / steal
beat / beet	hair / hare	pain / pane	sun / son
blue / blew	heel / heal	past / passed	tail / tale
break / brake	here / hear	peak / peek	tea / tee
by / buy / bye	hole / whole	rain / rein / reign	there / their / they're
days / daze	led / lead	red / read	to / too / two
dear / deer	maid / made	road / rode	way / weigh
do / dew	mail / male	roll / role	week / weak
die / dye	meet / meat	sea / see	wood / would

Homophone Phrases

peek at the peak	read the red book	see the sea
for four weeks	bare bear	be a bee
do not knot	ate eight berries	dear deer
hare with no hair	knew the new number	whole hole
break the brake	buy by the mall	heal his heel
our hour	fair fare	tale of a twisted tail

Homophone Sentences*

Rex rode his bicycle down the road.	We can see the sea from the house.
Bea would like to be a bee.	Bella blew up the blue balloon.
Don't break the brake on the bike.	It is not fair that the fare is so high.
Please do not tie the knot so tight.	Do you like to see the morning dew?
Dear deer, please do not eat the tender leaves.	The black bear had no fur and was bare.
Daisy spent the long hot days in a daze.	The horse went to the gate with a slow gait.
The long-eared hares had very little hair.	Howie's broken heel needs time to heal.
There is a hole in the whole doughnut.	Eight deer ate all the leaves in the garden.
Norris knew that the new suit was tight.	The hour has passed for dinner in our house.
We got a peek of the faraway mountain peak.	Robin read the red book to Roland.
So, can you sew some buttons on my shirt?	The sun shone directly in her son's eyes.
Ty told the tale of the dog with a twisty tail.	Willa would like to buy a boat made of wood.
I will write on the right sheet of paper.	They're going to their house over there.
Wanda felt weak from being sick all week.	The two toads hopped too many times.

* Note: You can present these sentences as "cloze" sentences. Using the words provided in parentheses, have children complete the sentence by filling in the appropriate word for each blank. For example: (blue, blew) Bella _____ up the _____ balloon.

Open Syllables

A *syllable* is a unit of pronunciation and usually contains one vowel sound. An *open syllable* ends in a vowel, as in the words *me* or *I*. The vowel sound is generally long and says its name because there are no consonants closing it in. You may start by introducing single-syllable words, but open syllables appear more commonly in two-syllable words, as in *ti-ger* or *ban-jo*.

Open Syllable Words

Open *e*	Open *i*	Open *o*	Open *u*	Open *y*
be	hi	go	flu	by
he	I	no		fly
me		so		my
she				sky
we				sly

Open Syllable Phrases

me or I	said "hi"	she and he
we or us	said "no"	can go
oh, my	had the flu	fly in the sky
a sly fox	fly by	my bag
fly up and up	the big sky	by and by

Open Syllable Sentences

He said hi to me.	We will go soon.
She said hi to him.	No, don't go.
I like you, and you like me.	We will be late.
We had the flu for just a day.	Oh, my, there's a fly in the sky.
He said "hi" and waved.	He and she can go to the market.
She said "no," and did not wave.	We can go see the kites fly.
He had the flu but got well soon.	So, we will go by the park.
Is it *me* or *I* at the start of a sentence?	Is it *we* or *us* at the end of a sentence?

V/CV Words

To decode multisyllabic words, children need to learn how to divide longer words into component syllables. This way, they can sound out each chunk and blend them back together. It is helpful to teach children the different syllabication patterns so they know where to properly divide words. The six basic syllable spelling patterns are:

1. **closed** – the syllable ends in a consonant (as in *pen-cil*)

2. **open** – the syllable ends in a vowel (as in *ve-to*)

3. **VCe** – the syllable represents the long-vowel sound (as in *lo-<u>cate</u>*)

4. *r*-**controlled** – the vowel and the *r* are in the same syllable (as in *pre-<u>fer</u>*)

5. **vowel team** – the syllable contains a vowel digraph (as in *re-<u>tain</u>*)

6. **C+*le*** – when *le* appears at the end of a word and is preceded by a consonant, the consonant and *le* make up the final syllable (as in *ta-<u>ble</u>*)

After children learn open syllables, they can transition to reading multisyllabic words with an initial open syllable, as in the word *ti-ger*. To divide a word into syllables, have children put dots under the vowels and look between the vowels. When there is one consonant between two vowels (VCV), one option is to divide the word before the consonant (V/CV). This makes the first syllable open and with a long-vowel sound, as in *pa-per*. Often, when the first syllable in a two-syllable word is open, the second syllable has a non-accented vowel pronounced with a schwa, as in *la-bel*.

> When *de-* is used as a prefix (meaning "down, away from, off"), the <u>first</u> syllable may have a schwa sound. Some words, such as *decode*, *deflate*, *decline*, and *delete*, exhibit this pattern.

V/CV Words

Open syllable + Closed syllable				
bacon	bonus	even	item	moment
basic	crocus	final	label	motel
basis	demand	frozen	legal	music*
begin	depend	hotel	lilac	open
belong	digest	human*	lotus	pilot
beyond	donut	Irish	minus	present

*The *u* ending in an open syllable may have a long-*u* /ū/ or a long-*oo* /o͞o/ sound.

Open syllable + Closed syllable *continued*				
prevent	student*	**gluten***	**oval**	**unit**
protect	tulip*	**haven**	**recent**	**vocal**
pupil*	**apex**	**humid***	**reject**	April
raven	**cubic**	**ibis**	**sequel**	duplex*
relax	**cupid***	**locust**	**sinus**	fragrant
result	**egret**	**navel**	**siren**	respect
robot	**eject**	**nasal**	**spiral**	sacred
rodent	**event**	**nomad**	**stamen**	secret
silent	**frequent**	**omit**	**tunic***	rubric*
Open syllable + VC*e* syllable				
behave	refile	**dilate**	**opine**	**remote**
create	refuse	**erode**	**ozone**	**revoke**
delete	relate	**evoke**	**placate**	**senile**
donate	rotate	**feline**	**predate**	**vacate**
erase	unite	**finite**	**presume**	microbes
female	**canine**	**futile**	**primate**	migrate
locate	**crusade**	**humane**	**profile**	recline
polite	**debate**	**irate**	**profuse**	vibrate
promote	**define**	**mutate**	**provoke**	
provide	**demote**	**notate**	**rebate**	

*The *u* ending in an open syllable may have a long-*u* /ū/ or a long-*oo* /o͞o/ sound.

In the V/CV pattern, some words may have an open first syllable while the second syllable begins with a consonant blend or digraph. For example, in the word *secret* the second syllable starts with the blend *cr*, while the second syllable of the word *gopher* starts with the digraph *ph*. See words in the shaded boxes.

Open syllable + *r*-Controlled syllable				
blazer	later	return	**caper**	**poker**
cider	major	rumor	**cedar**	**primer**
crater	motor	spider	**fiber**	**rotor**
diver	over	super	**labor**	**taper**
driver	paper	tiger	**meter**	**vapor**
favor	prefer	tutor	**minor**	**viper**
humor	refer		**plover**	gopher

Open syllable + C+*le* syllable				
able	cradle	stable	title	**ladle**
bugle	fable	staple	**bridle**	**noble**
cable	maple	table	**gable**	**trifle**

Open syllable + Open syllable				
baby	ivy	Pluto	wavy	**hazy**
cozy	lady	pony	yo-yo	**phony**
crazy	lazy	rhino	zero	**polo**
gravy	navy	solo	**ego**	**silo**
hero	photo	tidy	**halo**	**veto**
holy				

The Ultimate Book of Phonics Word Lists for Grades 1–2 © by Laurie J Cousseau and Rhonda Graff, Scholastic Inc.

V/CV Phrases

a pink tulip	ivy on the mailbox	a spider's web
zero to ten	planet Pluto	go solo
fuzzy spider	paper and fiber	super hero
secret haven	canine and feline	humid, hazy day
navy blazer	maple table	Felix the feline
bonus donuts	photo of the motel	apple cider
loud bugle	takes a photo	Greek fable
digest quickly	polite thank you	photo of the gopher

V/CV Sentences

Pablo will return the pliers later.	I love to relax with a good book.
Open the apple cider.	We sat at the maple table for dinner.
Ivy got gravy on her navy blazer.	Pluto rotates around its axis.
We got bonus donuts after the game.	Have you heard of the fable about a spider?
Davy prefers to play music on his banjo.	The canine and feline are recent friends.
The plate was made of paper and fiber.	Do you want tulips or lilacs in your garden?
On humid, hazy days, I like to be lazy.	There is a secret haven in the sequel.
Felix, the feline, is friends with the spider.	Let's return to the motel next to the crater.
Tatum will go solo on a secret crusade.	Count from zero to ten then take the photo.

VC/V Words

When there is one consonant between two vowels (VCV), we may divide after the consonant (VC/V). This makes the first syllable closed and with a short-vowel sound, as in *cam-el*. This is less common than V/CV, in which the first syllable is open (page 100). The second syllable may be closed or *r*-controlled. If the second syllable is closed, the vowel may have a non-accented schwa sound, as in *at-om*.

VC/V Words

Closed syllable + Closed syllable			
cabin	magic	satin	**Latin**
camel	melon	second	**lavish**
clinic	metal	seven	**method**
comic	model	solid	**panic**
denim	novel	topic	**rapid**
dragon	planet	travel	**relic**
edit	polish	vanish	**relish**
exam	present	visit	**rivet**
finish	product	wagon	**tepid**
habit	project	**atom**	**timid**
lemon	punish	**avid**	**tonic**
level	radish	**civic**	**tropic**
limit	robin	**comet**	**valid**
linen	salad	**credit**	**vivid**
Closed syllable + Open syllable			
banjo	lily	menu	memo
Closed syllable + VCe syllable			
tribune	tribute		

The Ultimate Book of Phonics Word Lists for Grades 1–2 © by Laurie J. Cousseau and Rhonda Graff, Scholastic Inc.

Closed syllable + r-Controlled syllable			
clever	desert	river	proper
cover			

VC/V Phrases

silver relic	lavish present	second planet
melon or lemon	denim jeans	project in the tropics
camel in the desert	cabin near the river	clever novel
yellow lily	hot desert	timid dragon
long exam	hungry robin	crunchy radish
rapid river	linen dress	on the menu

VC/V Sentences

We had lemons with our melons.	The model wore a linen dress.
The hungry robin hunted for food.	The timid dragon became my friend.
The rapid river runs very fast.	The cabin is next to the river.
The silver relic was a lavish gift.	The clever comic wore a satin vest.
A yellow lily bloomed in the desert.	The camel in the desert vanished!
They will finish building the cabin soon.	Venus is the second planet from the sun.
Gavin's denim jeans were bright blue.	We joined a research project in the tropics.
The clever novel was a tribute to planet Earth.	The covered wagon crossed the river.
Abby likes crunchy radishes in her salad.	Polish the silver spoon to make it shine.

Consonant + *le* Syllables

Consonant + *le* (C+*le*) is a final stable syllable; it always comes at the end of a word. The consonant may change, but the -*le* is always constant: -*ble*, -*cle*, -*dle*, -*fle*, -*gle*, -*kle*, -*ple*, and -*tle*. In the word *bubble*, the -*ble* is pronounced /bul/. In the word *ladle*, the -*dle* is pronounced /dul/. These words are Anglo-Saxon in origin and tend to be fairly basic vocabulary words. Children may get confused with other endings that sound similar to consonant + -*le*, such as -*el*, as in *novel*, and -*al*, as in *legal*.

Words such as *pebble* and *middle* have a double consonant in the middle because the consonant + *le* syllable is attached to a closed syllable. The first medial consonant closes in the vowel in the first syllable and "protects" the short-vowel sound. If there is only one consonant, the first syllable would be open and the vowel would not be protected. Therefore, the vowel would be long, and *pĕbble* would read as pē/ble and *mĭddle* would read as mī/dle. The second medial consonant is part of the consonant + *le* syllable.

Consonant + *le* (C+*le*) Words

Closed syllable + C+*le*			
apple	dimple	grumble	paddle
babble	dribble	handle	pebble
battle	drizzle	humble	puddle
bobble	duffle	jiggle	puzzle
bottle	fiddle	juggle	raffle
bubble	fizzle	jumble	rattle
bundle	fumble	kettle	riddle
candle	gaggle	little	ripple
cattle	gentle	middle	ruffle
crumble	giggle	mumble	saddle
crumple	gobble	nibble	scrabble
cuddle	goggles	nimble	scramble
dazzle	griddle	nozzle	settle

Closed syllable + C+le *continued*			
simple	thimble	**ample**	**kindle**
sizzle	topple	**brambles**	**muddle**
shuttle	tremble	**bumble**	**pimple**
snuggle	tumble	**dabble**	**quibble**
squiggle	uncle	**dwindle**	**ramble**
struggle	waffle	**gabble**	**rumble**
stumble	wiggle	**grapple**	**spindle**
tattle	wriggle	**haggle**	**straddle**

Open syllable + C+*le*			
able	fable	noble	**bridle**
bugle	idle	stable	**ogle**
cable	ladle	staple	**sable**
cradle	maple	table	**stifle**
cycle	Naples	title	**trifle**

Vowel team + C+*le*			
beagle	eagle	oodles	**feeble**
beetle	needle	poodle	**steeple**
doodle	noodle		**wheedle**

r-Controlled syllable + C+*le*			
article	sparkle	turtleneck	**gurgle**
circle	startle	**curdle**	**hurdle**
marble	tattle	**gargle**	**hurtle**
purple	turtle	**girdle**	

Consonant + *le* Phrases

mumble or babble	gentle cattle	duffle bag handle
smooth pebble	noble eagle	ping-pong paddle
glass bottle	kettle on the stove	hard puzzle
humble uncle	mud puddle	simple ruffle
rainy drizzle	juicy apple	ripple in the water
wriggle and jiggle	grumble and mumble	jumble of puzzle pieces
candle raffle	single waffle	middle of the castle
maple trifle	a noble deed	sharp staple
title of the fable	wooden cradle	horse stable
silver ladle	fancy table	charger cable
bald eagle	oodles of noodles	black beetles
beagles and poodles	sewing needle	tall steeple
purple circle	a tangle of cables	long article
startled turtle	shiny marble	over the last hurdle
purple beetle	scribble and doodle	speckled marble
castle in Naples	Jingle, the poodle	turtle in the puddle
pancakes on the griddle	able to unscramble	turtleneck with sparkles

Consonant + *le* Sentences

Stifle your sneeze at the table!	Are you able to play the bugle?
The boys scrambled up the hill.	Max began to juggle sparkly marbles.
They paddled down the long river.	I let go of the duffle bag handle.
The eagle perched on the steeple.	The runner cleared the last hurdle.
Would you want a beagle or poodle?	It is not polite to gobble the apple.
The jumble of brambles were a tangled mess!	Birds nestled in the middle of the apple tree.
The candle raffle was held at the castle.	The turtle splashed in the mud puddle.
Let's snuggle and settle in to read a story.	The ping-pong paddle flew under the table.
Have you ever heard a gaggle of geese giggle?	We scrambled up the hill then tumbled down.
Take off the horse's bridle at the stable.	Rock the cradle gently back and forth.
The trifle dessert tastes like maple syrup.	The noble gentleman wore a sable cloak.
The fable with the long title is about kindness.	Ladle the trifle into the bowls on the table.
Eagle babies are feeble when they hatch.	We want oodles of noodles for lunch.
We like to doodle pictures of poodles.	The puzzle pieces were jumbled on the table.
The shiny marbles rolled across the table.	Use the sewing needle to mend the tear.
The glass left a purple circle on the table.	The turtle gurgled as it slid into the water.
She wore a purple turtleneck with sparkles.	Gargle with salt water to help a sore throat.

Consonant + *le* Sentences *continued*	
His book is filled with scribbles and doodles.	The rumble of the thunder dwindled down.
The noble eagle flew over the vast jungle.	My humble uncle loves to play the fiddle.
The thistle flowers grew in a rambling hedge.	The gentle cattle wandered down to the water.
Jingle, the poodle, snuggled under the covers.	We arrived at the castle in the hotel shuttle.

Consonant + *le* can also be attached to a welded ending, such as *ng*, as in the words *jungle* and *tangle*, or *nk*, as in the words *wrinkle* and *ankle*. These are not always included in word lists for C+*le* words, but they are useful as they are a subset of words.

Welded Endings + Consonant + *le* Words

-ngle			
angle	jungle	tangle	**jangle**
bangle	rectangle	tingle	**mingle**
dangle	shingle	triangle	**wrangle**
jingle	single		

-nkle			
ankle	sprinkle	twinkle	**periwinkle**
crinkle	tinkle	wrinkle	**rankle**

For words that end in -stle, the t is silent, as in whistle. It is an Old English ending.

-stle			
castle	rustle	**bristle**	**jostle**
hustle	whistle	**bustle**	**thistle**
nestle	wrestle		

The Ultimate Book of Phonics Word Lists for Grades 1–2 © by Laurie J. Cousseau and Rhonda Graff, Scholastic Inc.

V/V Division Pattern

V/V is a division pattern in which two vowels are next to each other, but they do not present as a vowel team with a single sound. For example, the vowel team *ea* says /ē/ in *team*, and the vowel team *ai* says /ā/ in *wait*. In a V/V division pattern, however, the word is divided between the two vowels, and we pronounce both vowels, as in *li-on*. Often, the two vowels are not recognized as a vowel team. Sometimes the two vowels may look like a vowel team, but they don't behave as a vowel team, as in the words *du-et* or *po-et*.

V/V Words

boa	lion	quiet	**chaos**	**oasis**
create	meow	rodeo	**dual**	**prior**
cruel	museum	triangle	**fluent**	**riot**
diet	neon	video	**geometry**	**ruin**
duet	peony	violet	**iodine**	**stereo**
fluid	poem	violin	**mosaic**	**triumph**
giant	poet		**nucleus**	**vial**

V/V Phrases

giant lion	violin duet	violet peonies
fluent poet	video of a rodeo	triangles in geometry
a poem about a boa	vial of iodine	fluid dance
neon museum	oasis in the desert	neon lights

V/V Sentences

Joel wrote a poem about a quiet boa.	The vial of iodine can stain the floor.
Diana and Noel played a violin duet.	Can a lion say *meow*?
Romeo ate violet cookies at the museum.	Naomi likes to sing along with the violin.
We learned about triangles in geometry class.	Joshua made a video of the annual rodeo.
The vial of neon fluid glows in the dark.	Leo, the giant lion, loved to grow peonies.

Road Race

Players move along a game path as they search for words that contain target phonics skills.

Number of Players: 2 to 4

You'll Need: Road Race game board (pages 114–115) • Pit Stop Cards and Blank Game Cards (page 116) • scissors • tape • file folder (optional) • game pieces (e.g., buttons, coins) • pencils

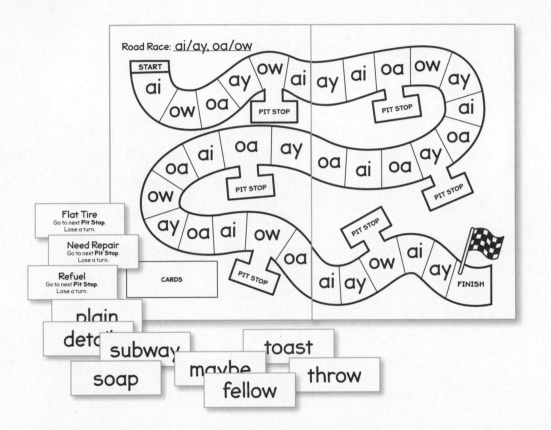

Setting Up the Game

Make a copy of the blank Road Race game board. Decide what phonetic pattern or skill you want children to practice. Fill in the letters or letter combinations on the blank line at the top of the game board so players know their options when completing the game cards. **Note:** Consider choosing skills that require children to recognize positional differences or distinct patterns. Vowel teams work well. For example, you may want to focus on *ai* and *ay*, emphasizing the position of each vowel team in a word. In each space on the game board, write one of the letter combinations being highlighted.

To assemble the game board, fold or cut along the dotted line (B), and tape (B) to (A) as indicated. (Optional: Glue or tape the game board to the inside of a file folder to make it sturdier.)

Photocopy the Pit Stop Cards and Blank Game Cards onto cardstock. Make as many copies of the blank game cards as needed. Find the corresponding word lists in the book and choose words for the game. Write the words on the cards, leaving off the part of the word that includes the focus skill. Players will decide what letters are needed to complete the word. (For example, if you write *st___* on the card, players will fill in the missing *ay* for *stay*.)

Cut apart all the game cards, including the Pit Stop Cards. Shuffle the cards together and stack them face down on the Cards box on the game board. Provide pencils and game pieces for each player.

How to Play

1. Players take turns picking a card from the top of the CARD pile.
   - If players get a word card, they decide what letters are missing in the word and write in those letters. Then, players move their game piece to the first spot on the game board with those missing letters and read aloud the word.
   - If players get a Pit Stop Card, they move to the next Pit Stop space and lose a turn.
2. Players continue taking turns until a player reaches FINISH.
3. The first player to reach FINISH wins the game.

Going Further

For additional practice, make extra copies of the game board for children to take home and play with their families.

Road Race: _____

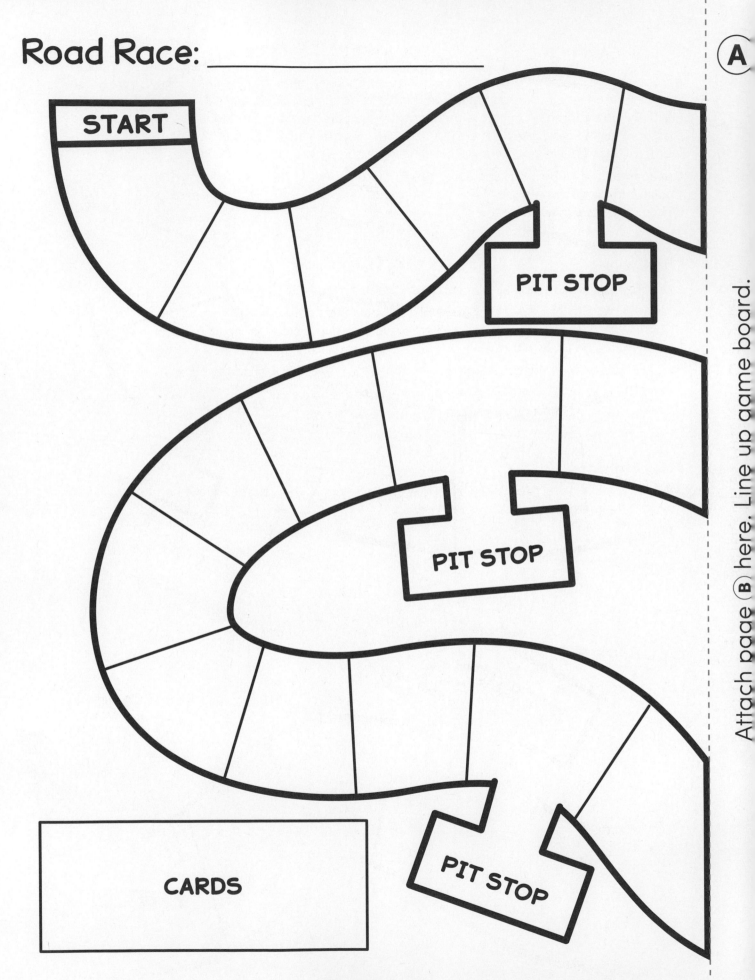

START

PIT STOP

PIT STOP

PIT STOP

CARDS

Attach page Ⓑ here. Line up game board.

Fold or cut on dotted line. Attach to page A.

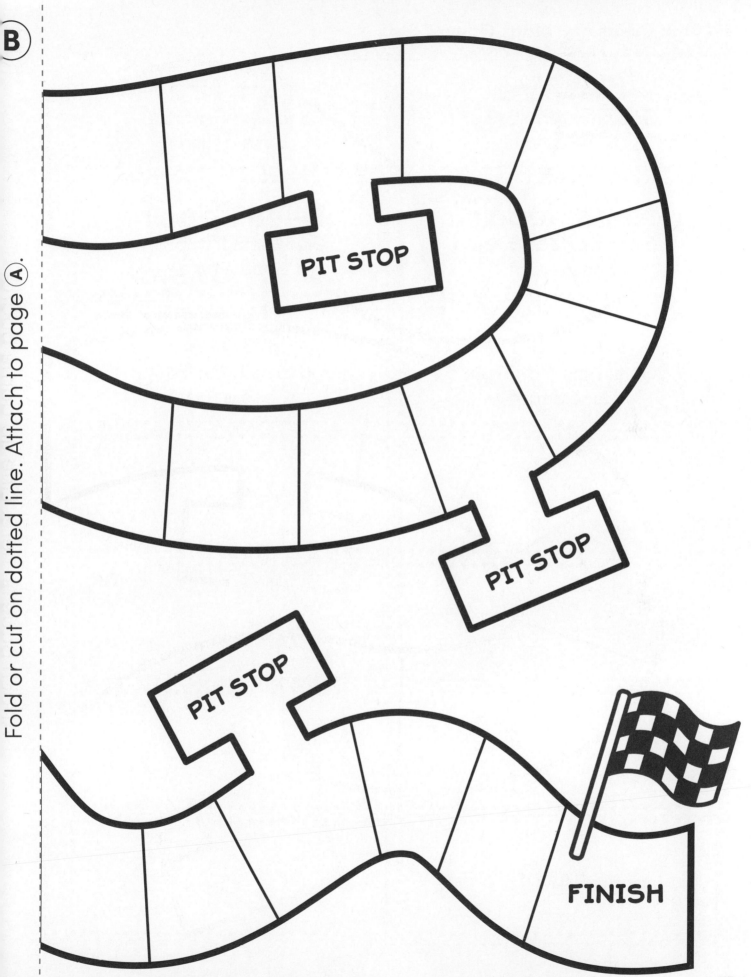

PIT STOP

PIT STOP

PIT STOP

FINISH

Flat Tire
Go to next **Pit Stop**.
Lose a turn.

Flat Tire
Go to next **Pit Stop**.
Lose a turn.

Need Repair
Go to next **Pit Stop**.
Lose a turn.

Need Repair
Go to next **Pit Stop**.
Lose a turn.

Refuel
Go to next **Pit Stop**.
Lose a turn.

Refuel
Go to next **Pit Stop**.
Lose a turn.

The Ultimate Book of Phonics Word Lists for Grades 1–3 © by Laurie 1 Cousseau and Rhonda Graff Scholastic Inc.

Star Words

Use this word-building activity for the whole class, small groups, or independent practice.

You'll Need: Star Words activity sheet (page 118) • pencils

Setting Up the Game

Make a copy of the Star Words activity sheet. Decide what phonetic pattern or skill you want children to practice (for example, *r*-controlled vowels). Write the focus pattern/skill in the star at the center of the page. Find the corresponding word lists in the book and choose words for the game.

At the bottom part of the sheet, fill in the blanks with letters that, when combined with the highlighted pattern, will form actual words. It is important to brainstorm words first to choose letters that will allow children to create the most words with the focus phonetic pattern. Choose letters that can be used in multiple words.

Then, make a copy of the activity sheet for each child.

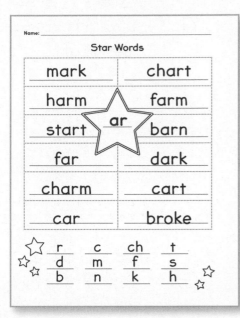

How to Play

1. Children use the phonetic pattern in the star and the letters at the bottom of the page to make words. They may use only the focus pattern and the letters on the page. Every word must include the focus phonetic pattern.

2. Children build words and write them on the lines around the star on the activity sheet.

3. When children have completed their activity sheet, invite them to share their words.

Going Further

For additional practice, make extra copies of the activity sheet for children to take home and work on with their families.

Name: _____

Star Words

The Ultimate Book of Phonics Word Lists for Grades 1–2 © by Laurie J. Cousseau and Rhonda Graff. Scholastic Inc.

Pizza Spinner Game

In this strategic game, children try to get three words with the same spelling pattern in a row without getting blocked by the other player.

Number of Players: 2

You'll Need: Pizza Spinner and Pizza Box sheet (page 120) • Pizza Peel Chart (page 121) • pencil and paper clip (for the spinner) • pencil for each player

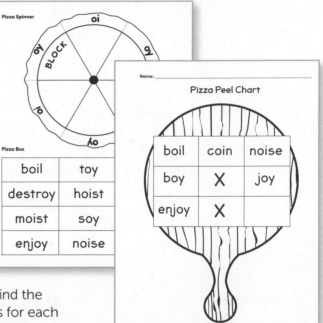

Setting Up the Game

Make a copy of the blank Pizza Spinner and Pizza Box sheet. Decide what phonetic patterns or skills you want children to practice (for example, diphthongs). Write the spelling patterns (for example, *oi* and *oy*) along the edge of the pizza crust. Find the corresponding word lists in the book and choose words for each spelling pattern (12 words in all). Write the words in the blank spaces on the Pizza Box.

For the Pizza Spinner, provide players with a pencil and paper clip to use as a spinner. Model how to use the spinner: Hold the pencil upright at the center of the spinner. Place the paper clip at the bottom of the pencil. With your fingers, flick the paper clip to use it as a spinner.

Make a copy of the Pizza Peel Chart for each player. Give each player a pencil.

How to Play

1. Each player gets a Pizza Peel Chart.

2. Players take turns spinning the spinner. Depending on where the spinner lands, players choose a word from the Pizza Box that has that specific spelling pattern. For example, if players land on *oi*, they can choose any of the *oi* words.

3. Players write their chosen word on their Pizza Peel Chart. The goal is to get three words in a row with the same phonetic pattern.

4. If players land on BLOCK, they have two choices:

   • The player can play as usual by picking a word with the spelling pattern on that slice of pizza and fill in his or her Pizza Peel Chart accordingly.

   • The player can "block" the other player by placing an *X* on their opponent's Pizza Peel Chart. An *X* in a box means it cannot be used for a word.

5. The first player to get three words with the same spelling pattern in a row—horizontally, vertically, or diagonally—wins. The player must read all three words correctly to win.

Going Further

For additional practice, make extra copies of the Pizza Spinner and Pizza Box sheet and Pizza Peel Chart for children to take home and play with their families.

Pizza Spinner

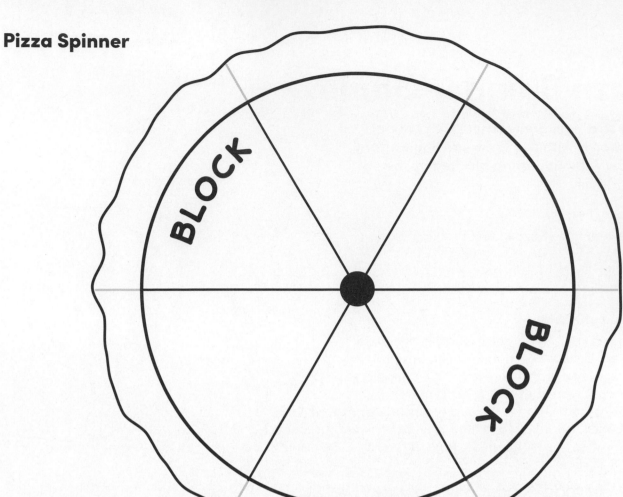

Pizza Box

The Ultimate Book of Phonics Word Lists for Grades 1–2 © by Laurie 1 Cousseau and Rhonda Graff. Scholastic Inc.

Pizza Peel Chart

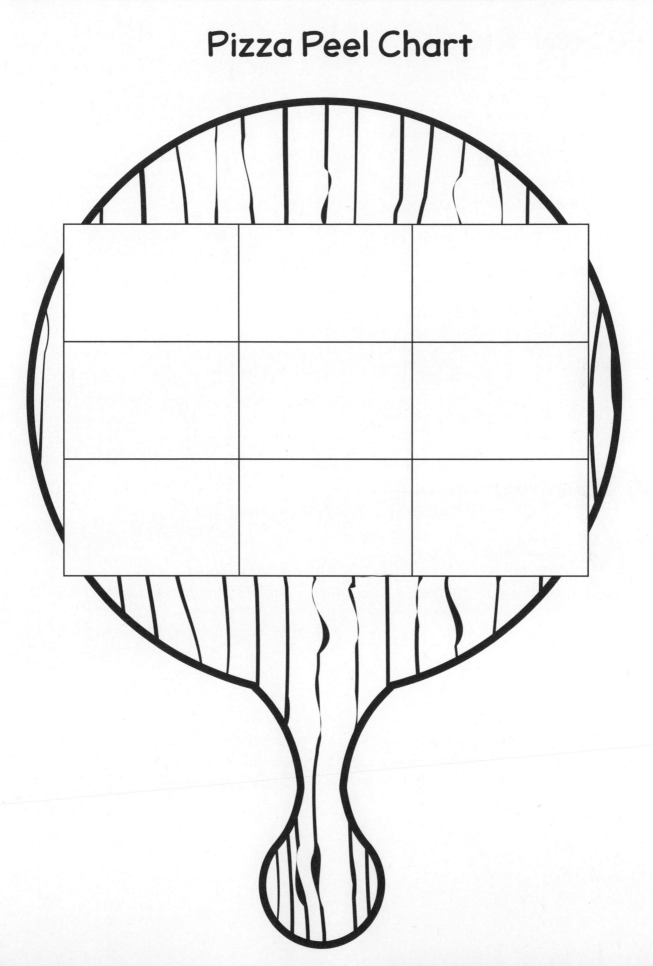

Four Block

Give children practice in building fluency as they read columns of words while trying to build a Four Block of connecting boxes.

Number of Players: 2

You'll Need: Four Block game board (page 123) • number cube • crayons or colored pencils

Setting Up the Game

Make a copy of the blank Four Block game board. Decide what phonetic pattern or skill you want children to practice (for example, *y* as a vowel). Find the corresponding word lists in the book and choose words for the activity. Write the words in the blank spaces on the activity sheet. Then, make a copy for each player. Have each player choose a colored crayon or pencil to use during the game.

Four Block

Name: _____

Roll the number cube. Find the column with the same number. Read the words in that column. Then, color in a box from that column. The goal is to color in four boxes that touch.

1	2	3	4	5	6
funny	pry	fancy	jelly	fuzzy	penny
by	hobby	sty	lady	dusty	granny
candy	cry	my	sky	pony	soapy
shy	chilly	kitty	snowy	stormy	sly
messy	rusty	fly	wavy	why	tidy
lucky	fry	spicy	dry	tiny	sticky

Challenge: Choose a word. Use it in a sentence.

How to Play

1. Players take turns rolling a number cube to see which column of words to read.

2. At their turn, players read all the words in that column. (Have an adult check for accuracy.)

3. After players finish reading their word list, they use their crayon or pencil to color in one box from that column. The goal is to color in four boxes that touch to create a square, or a continuous four-box row, column, or diagonal.

4. Players continue taking turns until there are no more boxes left to color in to make a block of four.

5. The player who has the most blocks of four wins.

Going Further

- Challenge players to pick a word from a column and use it in a sentence.
- Allow players to read the list from top to bottom or from bottom to top.
- For additional practice, make extra copies of the game board for children to take home and play with their families.

Four Block

Name: _____

Roll the number cube. Find the column with the same number. Read the words in that column. Then, color in a box from that column. The goal is to color in four boxes that touch.

1	2	3	4	5	6

Challenge: Choose a word. Use it in a sentence.

Fluency Voices

Add drama and excitement to fluency practice with this activity that challenges children to read a list of words using different voices.

Number of Players: 2

You'll Need: Fluency Voices activity sheet (page 125) • 2 paper clips • number cube

Setting Up the Game

Make a copy of the blank Fluency Voices activity sheet. Decide what phonetic pattern or skill you want children to practice (for example, soft *c*). Find the corresponding word lists in the book and choose words for the activity. Write the words in the blank spaces on the sheet. Then make as many copies of the actiivty sheet as needed.

Place one paper clip along the left edge of the sheet and another paper clip along its right edge. Each player slides the paper clip up or down the list to highlight the word they are reading.

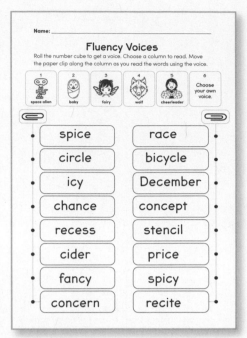

How to Play

1. Players take turns rolling a number cube to get a character on the top of the page.

2. At their turn, players choose a column of words to read, using the voice of their given character. Players move the paper clip up or down the list as they read each word on the list.

3. Players continue taking turns until each child has read each column using at least three different voices or until a specified time limit has been met.

Going Further

For additional practice, make extra copies of the activity sheet for children to take home and play with their families.

Name: _____

Fluency Voices

Roll the number cube to get a voice. Choose a column to read. Move
the paper clip along the column as you read the words using the voice.

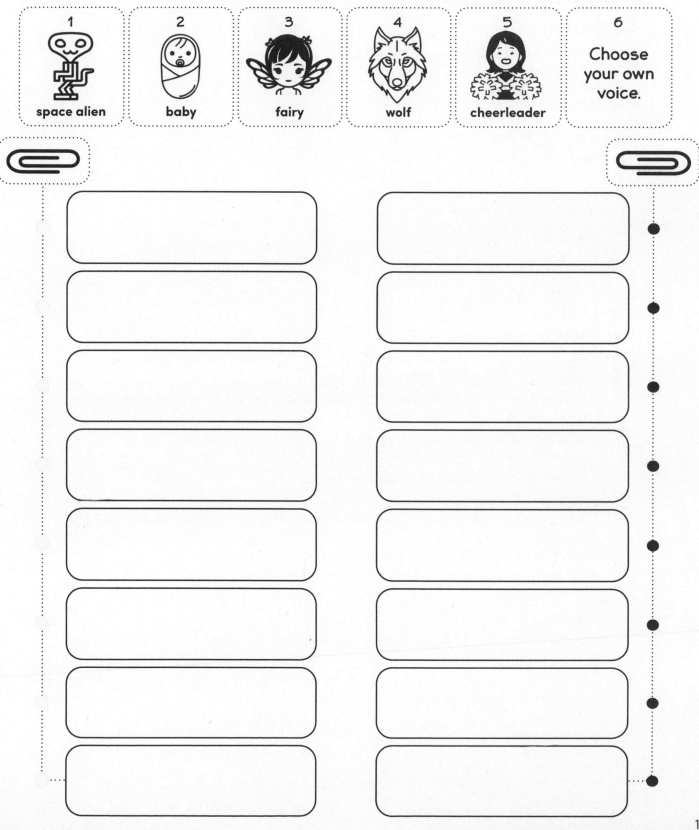

1	2	3	4	5	6
space alien	baby	fairy	wolf	cheerleader	Choose your own voice.

Build-a-Contraction

In this exciting, skill-building game, players pick word cards to try to build a contraction.

Number of Players: 2

You'll Need: Build-a-Contraction game board (page 127) • Build-a-Contraction game cards and Award Ribbons (page 128) • Contractions word lists (page 84)

Setting Up the Game

Make a copy of the blank Build-a-Contraction game board and game cards. Use the Contractions word list to choose five contractions for the game. On the blank game cards, write the contractions and the two words that make up each contraction (for a total of 15 word cards). Cut all the cards apart, including the five Award Ribbon cards.

Build-a-Contraction Game Board Name: _____

Words		Contraction
can	not	can't
they		they'll
	is	what's
I		I've
	are	you're

will
not
you're

How to Play

1. Shuffle the game cards and stack them face down near the game board. Place the Award Ribbon cards on the side.

2. Players take turns picking a card from the stack.
   - If players pick one of the words that make up a contraction, they place the card on the game board under "Words."
   - If players pick a contraction, they place the card on the game board under "Contraction."
   - The goal is to complete each row with two word cards and their matching contraction.

3. Players continue picking game cards and filling up the board. When players place a card on the board that completes a row (two words and their contraction), they must read all three parts to earn an Award Ribbon.

4. The player with the most Award Ribbons at the end of the game wins.

Going Further

- Customize the game by creating your own game cards to target other skills, such building compound words.
- For additional practice, make extra copies of the game board and cards for children to take home and play with their families.

The Ultimate Book of Phonics Word Lists for Grades 1–2 © by Laurie J. Cousseau and Rhonda Graff. Scholastic Inc.

Build-a-Contraction
Game Board

Name: _____

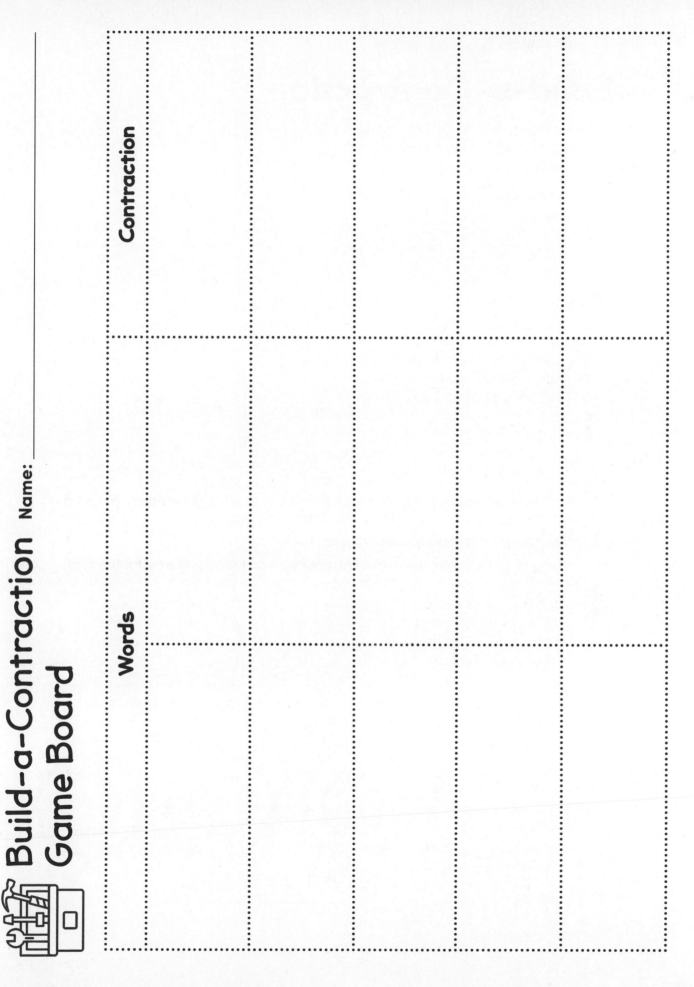

Words	Contraction

Build-a-Contraction Game Cards

Fill in the blank cards with five contractions and the two words
that make up each contraction.

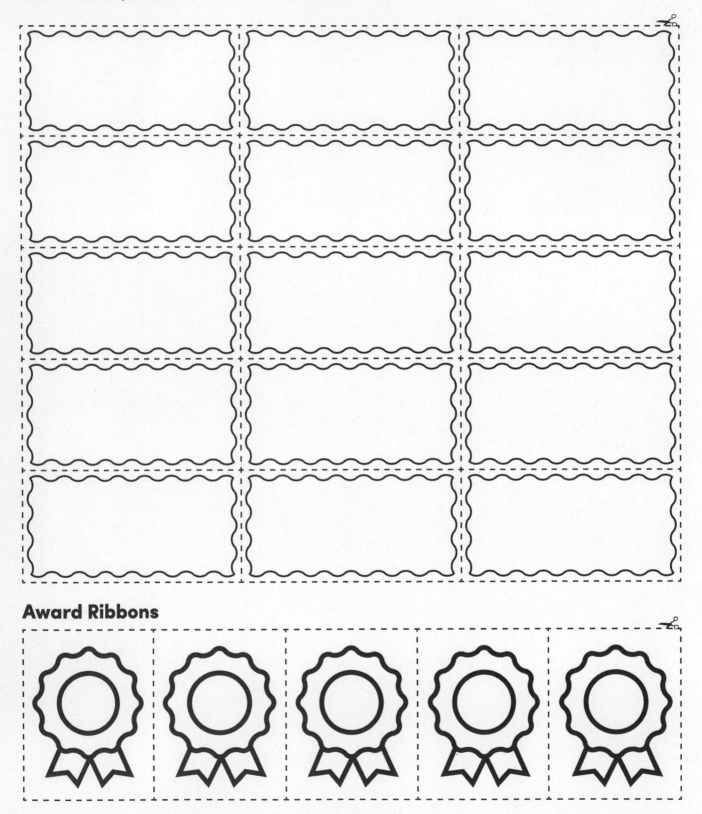

Award Ribbons

The Ultimate Book of Phonics Word Lists for Grades 1–2 © by Laurie J. Cousseau and Rhonda Graff, Scholastic Inc.

Blooming Spelling Rules

Use these activity sheets to reinforce the three suffix spelling rules. Each suffix spelling rule comes with two levels of activities: Level 1 helps children learn the spelling rule, and Level 2 provides practice with the rule. These activities can be used by individuals or pairs of players.

Suffix Spelling Rule #1: Drop *e*

Level 1 (Learn the Rule)

Number of Players: 1 or 2

You'll Need: Drop *e* Flower (page 131) • Drop *e* Words (pages 86–87) • Base Words Columns (page 132) • Suffix Cards (page 133) • Suffix Spelling Worksheet (page 134) • pencils

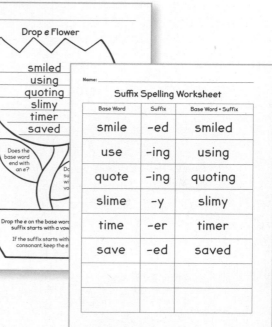

Setting Up the Game

Make a copy of the Drop *e* Flower activity sheet for each child or pair of children.

Next, make a copy of the blank Base Words Columns. Using the corresponding Drop *e* Words in the book, fill in the blanks with base words that will work with the Drop *e* spelling rule. Cut apart the Base Word Columns and spread the three columns face up on the table so all the words are visible to the players.

Then, make one or two copies of the Suffix Cards. (Note: The last column of cards is blank so you can fill them in with other suffixes, if you wish.) Make sure the suffixes and base words are compatible. Cut apart the Suffix Cards and stack them face down in a pile.

How to Play

1. Players take turns picking a Suffix Card from the stack.

2. Players look at the Base Words Columns to see if they can pair the suffix with a base word.

3. Using the Drop *e* Flower page, players review the checkpoints on the leaves for the Drop *e* spelling rule. (Encourage children to go through each checkpoint, especially while they are still learning the spelling rule.)

4. Players write the word (base word + suffix) on the lines in the flower.

5. When all the lines on the flower have been filled in, players read all the words.

Encourage children to use the Suffix Spelling Worksheet to write the base words and suffixes while they are still learning the suffix spelling rules. It is a useful visual to help them work through the checkpoints of each rule.

Level 2 (Apply the Rule)

After children have learned the Drop *e* rule, they need to decide whether the rule applies to a base word. Level 2 provides application practice.

Number of Players: 1 or 2

You'll Need: Drop *e* Flower (page 131) • Drop *e* Words (pages 86–87) • Base Word + Suffix Strips (page 135) • Suffix Spelling Worksheet (page 134) • scissors • pencils

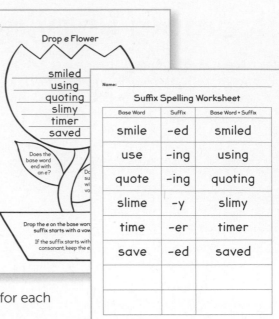

Setting up the Game

Make a copy of the Drop *e* Flower activity sheet for each child or pair of children.

Next, make a copy of the blank Base Word + Suffix Strips. Using the corresponding Drop *e* Words in the book, fill in the blanks with base words and suffixes. Include both vowel and consonant suffixes, allowing children to determine when to keep and when to drop the *e*. Cut apart the Base Word + Suffix Strips and place them face down in a pile.

How to Play

1. Players take turns picking a strip from the pile.

2. At their turn, players decide how to spell the word formed by joining the base word and suffix on the strip. Players can use the checkpoints on the Drop *e* Flower leaves to decide whether the rule applies to the base word. Encourage them to use the Suffix Spelling Worksheet, if needed.

3. If the Drop *e* rule applies, players write the word on the flower. If the rule does not apply, players explain why.

4. When all the lines on the flower have been filled in, players read all the words.

Going Further

- Consider making a self-checking answer key so children can check their work independently.

- Offer opportunities for children to work in reverse. Provide them with the whole word and have them isolate the base word and suffix. When they write the base word, the final *e* that was "dropped" will go back on the base word. Children need to recognize this and practice it.

- For additional practice, make extra copies of the activity sheet for children to take home and work on with their families.

Name: _____

Drop *e* Flower

Does the base word end with an *e*?

Does the suffix begin with a vowel?

Drop the *e* on the base word if the suffix starts with a vowel.

If the suffix starts with a consonant, keep the *e*.

Base Words Columns

The Ultimate Book of Phonics Word Lists for Grades 1–2 © by Laurie 1 Cousseau and Rhonda Graff, Scholastic Inc.

Suffix Cards

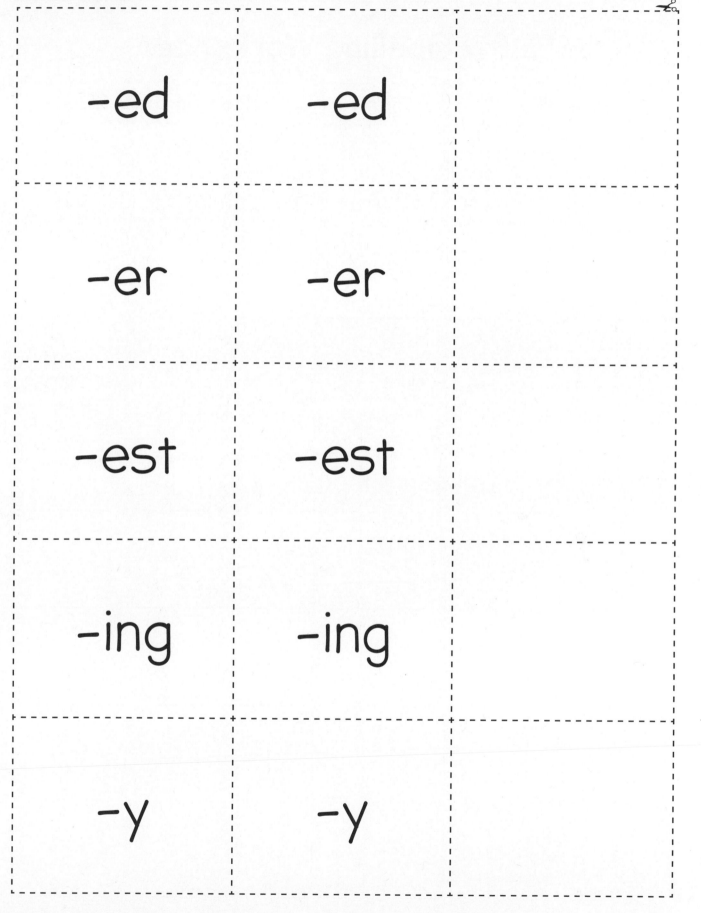

-ed	-ed	
-er	-er	
-est	-est	
-ing	-ing	
-y	-y	

Name: _____

Suffix Spelling Worksheet

Base Word	Suffix	Base Word + Suffix

The Ultimate Book of Phonics Word Lists for Grades 1–2 © by Laurie J. Cousseau and Rhonda Graff, Scholastic Inc.

Base Word + Suffix Strips

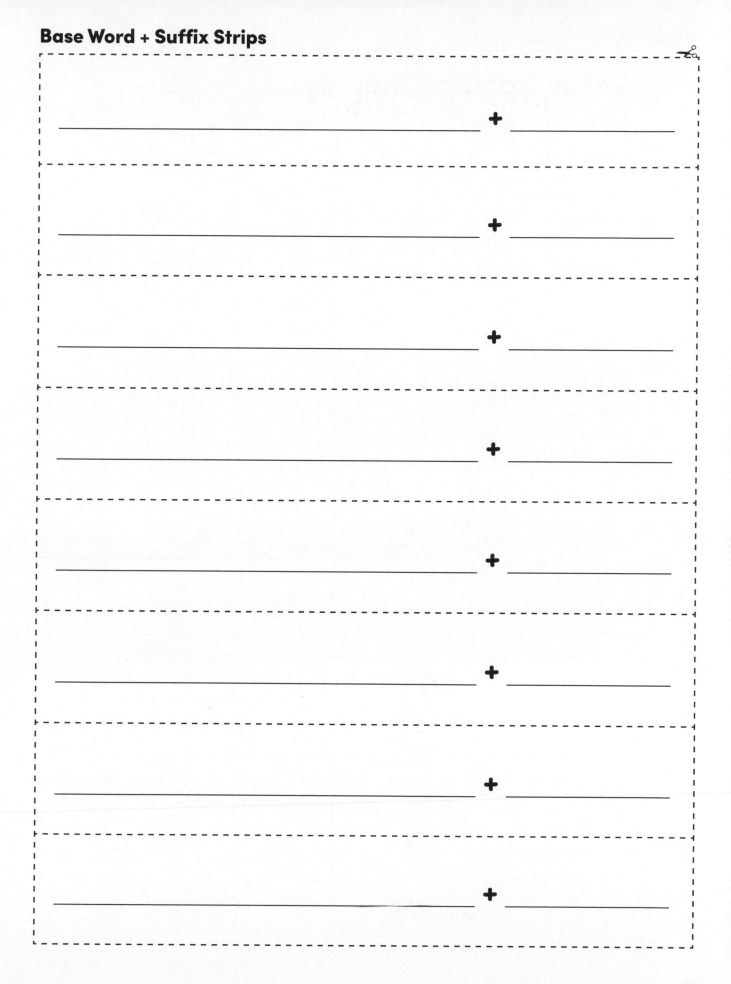

Suffix Spelling Rule #2: Double the Final Consonant

Level 1 (Learn the Rule)

Number of Players: 1 or 2

You'll Need: Double the Final Consonant Flower (page 138) • Double the Final Consonant Words (pages 91–92) • Base Words Columns (page 132) • Suffix Cards (page 133) • Suffix Spelling Worksheet (page 134) • pencils

Setting up the Game

Make a copy of the Double the Final Consonant Flower activity sheet for each child or pair of children.

Next, make a copy of the blank Base Words Columns. Using the corresponding Double the Final Consonant Words in the book, fill in the blanks with base words that will work with the Double the Final Consonant spelling rule. Then, cut apart the Base Word Columns and spread the three columns face up on the table so all the words are visible to the players.

Finally, make one or two copies of the Suffix Cards. (Note: The last column of cards is blank so you can fill them in with other suffixes, if you wish.) Make sure the suffixes and base words are compatible. Cut apart the Suffix Cards and stack them face down in a pile.

How to Play

1. Players take turns picking a Suffix Card from the stack.

2. Players look at the Base Words List to see if they can pair the suffix with a base word.

3. Using Double the Final Consonant Flower page, players review the checkpoints on the petals for the Double the Final Consonant spelling rule. (Encourage children to go through each checkpoint, especially while they are still learning the spelling rule.)

4. Players write the word (base word + suffix) on the lines in the flowerpot.

5. When all the lines on the flowerpot have been filled in, players read all the words.

Double the Final Consonant Flower

1. Is the base word one syllable?
2. Does the base word have a single short vowel?
3. Does the base word end with a single consonant?
4. Does the suffix begin with a vowel?

spinner
sitting
foggy
thinnest
tapped

Suffix Spelling Worksheet

Base Word	Suffix	Base Word + Suffix
spin	-er	spinner
sit	-ing	sitting
fog	-y	foggy
thin	-est	thinnest
tap	-ed	tapped

Level 2 (Apply the Rule)

After children have learned the Double the Final Consonant rule, they need to decide whether the rule applies to a base word. Level 2 provides application practice.

Number of Players: 1 or 2

You'll Need: Double the Final Consonant Flower (page 138) • Double the Final Consonants Words (pages 91–92) • Base Word + Suffix Strips (page 135) • Suffix Spelling Worksheet (page 134) • scissors • pencils

Setting Up the Game

Make a copy of the Double the Final Consonant Flower activity sheet for each child or pair of children.

Next, make a copy of the blank Base Word + Suffix Strips. Using the corresonding Double the Final Consonants Words in the book, fill in the blanks with base words and suffixes that require doubling and base words and suffixes that do <u>not</u> require doubling. This allows children to determine when to double the consonant and when to leave it as a single consonant. Cut apart the Base Word + Suffix Strips and place them face down in a pile.

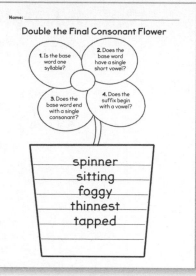

Name: _____

Double the Final Consonant Flower

1. Is the base word one syllable?
2. Does the base word have a single short vowel?
3. Does the base word end with a single consonant?
4. Does the suffix begin with a vowel?

spinner
sitting
foggy
thinnest
tapped

How to Play

1. Players take turns picking a strip from the pile.

2. At their turn, players decide how to spell the word formed by joining the base word and suffix on the strip. Players can use the checkpoints on the Double the Final Consonant Flower petals to decide whether the rule applies to the base word. Encourage them to use the Suffix Spelling Worksheet, if needed.

3. If the Double the Final Consonant rule applies, players write the word on the flowerpot. If the rule does not apply, players explain why.

4. When all the lines on the flowerpot have been filled in, players read all the words.

Going Further

- Consider making a self-checking answer key so children can check their work independently.

- Provide opportunities for children to work in reverse. Provide them with the whole word and have them isolate the base word and suffix. When they write the base word, the consonant that was doubled in the Double the Final Consonant rule will drop. Children need to recognize this and practice it.

- For additional practice, make extra copies of the activity sheet for children to take home and play with their families.

Double the Final Consonant Flower

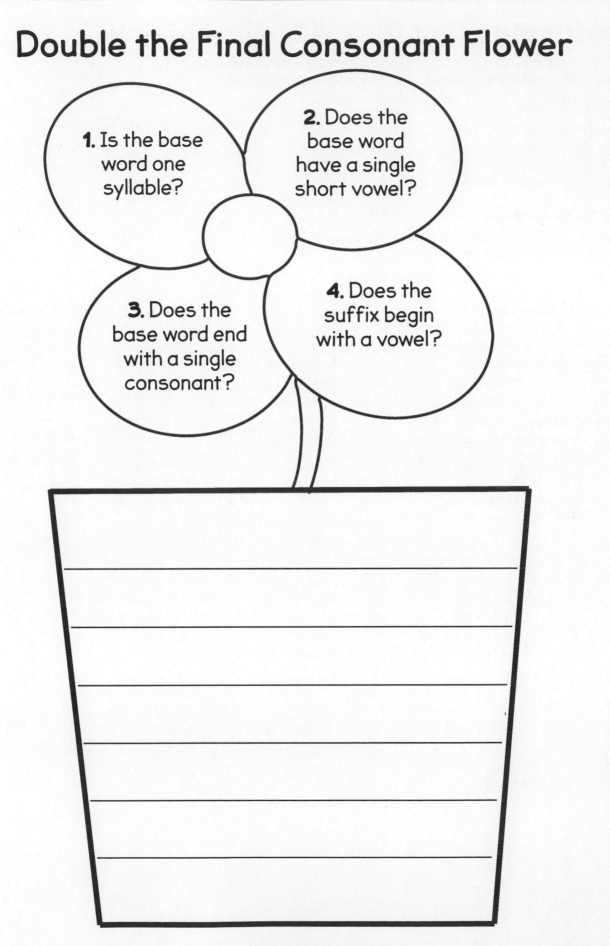

1. Is the base word one syllable?

2. Does the base word have a single short vowel?

3. Does the base word end with a single consonant?

4. Does the suffix begin with a vowel?

Suffix Spelling Rule #3: Change *y* to *i*

Level 1 (Learn the Rule)

Number of Players: 1 or 2

You'll Need: Change *y* to *i* Flower (page 141) • Change *y* to *i* Word Lists (pages 94–95) • Base Words Columns (page 132) • Suffix Cards (page 133) • Suffix Spelling Worksheet (page 134) • pencils

Setting Up the Game

Make a copy of the Change *y* to *i* Flower activity sheet for each child or pair of children.

Next, make a copy of the blank Base Words Columns. Using the corresponding Change *y* to *i* Words in the book, fill in the blanks with base words that will work with the Change *y* to *i* spelling rule. Then, cut apart the Base Word Columns and spread the three columns face up on the table so all the words are visible to the players.

Finally, make one or two copies of the Suffix Cards. (Note: The last column of cards is blank so you can fill them in with other suffixes, if you wish.) Make sure the suffixes and base words are compatible. Cut apart the Suffix Cards and stack them face down in a pile.

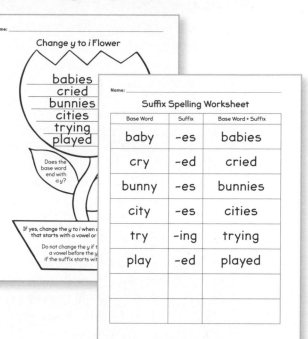

How to Play

1. Players take turns picking a Suffix Card from the stack.

2. Players look at the Base Words Columns to see if they can pair the suffix with a base word.

3. Using the Change *y* to *i* Flower page, players review the checkpoints on the leaves for the Change *y* to *i* spelling rule. (Encourage children to go through each checkpoint, especially while they are still learning the spelling rule.)

4. Players write the word (base word + suffix) on the lines on the flower.

5. When all the lines on the flower have been filled in, players read all the words.

Level 2 (Apply the Rule)

After children have learned the Change *y* to *i* rule, they need to decide whether the rule applies to a base word. Level 2 provides application practice.

Number of Players: 1 or 2

You'll Need: Change *y* to *i* Flower (page 141) • Change *y* to *i* Words (pages 94–95) • Base Word + Suffix Strips (page 135) • Suffix Spelling Worksheet (page 134) • scissors • pencils

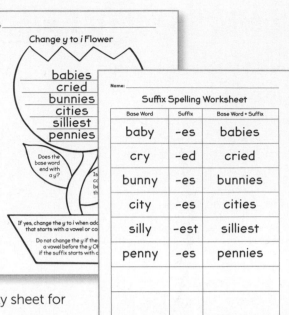

Setting Up the Game

Make a copy of the Change *y* to *i* Flower activity sheet for each child or pair of children.

Next, make a copy of the blank Base Word + Suffix Strips. Using the corresponding Change *y* to *i* Words in the book, fill in the blanks with base words and suffixes that require the Change *y* to *i* spelling rule and base words and suffixes that do <u>not</u> require any change to the base word. This allows children to determine when to change the *y* to *i* and when to simply add the suffix. Cut apart the Base Word + Suffix Strips and place them face down in a pile.

How to Play

1. Players take turns picking a strip from the pile.

2. At their turn, players decide how to spell the word formed by joining the base word and suffix on the strip. Players can use the checkpoints on the Change *y* to *i* Flower leaves to decide whether the rule applies to the base word. Encourage them to use the Suffix Spelling Worksheet, if needed.

3. If the Change *y* to *i* rule applies, players write the word on the flower. If the rule does not apply, players explain why.

4. When all the lines on the flower have been filled, players read all the words.

Going Further

- Consider making a self-checking answer key so children can check their work independently.

- Provide opportunities for children to work in reverse. Provide them with the whole word and have them isolate the base word and suffix. The *y* that changed to an *i* will go back to a *y* on the base word. Children need to recognize this and practice it.

- Provide children with a list of words that includes all three suffix spelling rules. Have them sort the words by the spelling rules. Always encourage them to explain why they chose to spell a word or sort a word in a certain way.

- For additional practice, make extra copies of the activity sheet for children to take home and play with their families.

Name: _____

Change *y* to *i* Flower

Does the base word end with a *y*?

Is there a consonant before the *y*?

If yes, change the *y* to *i* when adding a suffix that starts with a vowel or consonant.

Do not change the *y* if there is a vowel before the *y* OR if the suffix starts with an *i*.

Syllable Sandwiches

This word-sort activity is perfect for independent practice.

You'll Need: Syllable Sandwiches activity sheet (page 143) • Menu Sort sheet (page 144) • colored pencils or crayons • index card (optional)

Setting Up the Game

Make a copy of the blank Syllable Sandwiches and Menu Sort sheets. (If you wish to include more words for the sort, make multiple copies of the Syllable Sandwiches page.) Choose specific syllabication patterns for children to sort (for example, open syllables and closed syllables). At the top of the Menu Sort sheet, fill in the two column headers with the syllabication patterns.

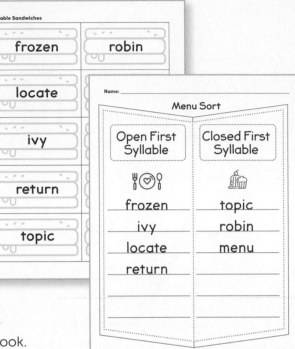

Next, find the corresponding word lists in the book. Fill the sandwiches with words that highlight the syllabication patterns you chose. Make sure to leave space between each letter in the words so children can divide the words as needed. Make a copy of the completed Syllable Sandwiches and Menu Sort sheets for each child. Provide children with colored pencils or crayons to mark the place of syllabication.

On a separate index card, consider writing the syllabication patterns as a reminder for children. Also, consider making an answer key so players can check their work independently.

How to Play

1. Each child gets a Syllable Sandwiches page and a Menu Sort page.

2. On the Syllable Sandwiches page, children divide the words based on the syllabication patterns introduced. Children use the colored pencils to mark where the syllable divides.

3. Next, children sort the words on the Menu Sort page.

4. Children share their sorts, reading the words in each column. Discuss why each word belongs in a particular column.

Going Further

For additional practice, make extra copies of the activity sheets for children to take home and play with their families. This versatile handout can be used to sort single-syllable types, such as closed syllables and V-*e* syllables, or for any sorting activity.

The Ultimate Book of Phonics Word Lists for Grades 1–2 © by Laurie J. Cousseau and Rhonda Graff. Scholastic Inc.

Syllable Sandwiches

Name: _____

Menu Sort

144

The Ultimate Book of Phonics Word Lists for Grades 1–2 © by Laurie J. Cousseau and Rhonda Graff, Scholastic Inc.